Queer Between the Covers

Histories of Queer Publishing and Publishing Queer Voices

This book is respectfully dedicated to the nine named defendants, living and dead, in Operation Tiger, the state's illegitimate attack on Gay's the Word, and by extension queer books and queer lives. They have a worthy place in a long and sadly ongoing resistance, and we owe them a great deal:

Charles Brown
Jonathan Cutbill
Peter Dorey
John Duncan
Paud Hegarty
Lesley Jones
Glenn McKee
Amanda Russell
Gerard Walsh

Queer Between the Covers

Histories of Queer Publishing and Publishing Queer Voices

Edited by Leila Kassir and Richard Espley

SENATE HOUSE LIBRARY
UNIVERSITY OF LONDON PRESS

Senate House Library
University of London
Senate House
Malet Street
London
WC1E 7HU

https://london.ac.uk/press

University of London Press, 2021

This book is also available online at https://humanities-digital-library.org/.

ISBN 978-1-913002-04-6 (Paperback edition)
ISBN 978-1-913002-05-3 (PDF edition)
ISBN 978-1-913002-06-0 (EPUB edition)
ISBN 978-1-913002-07-7 (Kindle edition)

Cover image by Mark Mitchell

UNIVERSITY OF LONDON PRESS | SENATE HOUSE LIBRARY

Contents

List of figures

Notes on contributors

Jennifer Dentel is an independent researcher and curator from Chicago. Jennifer currently works at Gerber/Hart, an LGBTQ library and archive specializing in the LGBTQ history and culture of Chicago and the Midwest. In addition to her research on pulp author and activist Valerie Taylor, she has co-curated several exhibits at Gerber/Hart, including on pre-Stonewall activism, the history of drag in Chicago, and lesbians and feminism in Chicago in the 1970s and '80s.

Jeremy Dixon is a poet and founder of groundbreaking queer publishing house Hazard Press, based in Wales. Jeremy is also a designer and lecturer on book arts. He has participated in book fairs including Turn the Page in Norwich and the Small Publishers' Fair in London. His debut poetry collection *IN RETAIL* was published by Arachne Press in February 2019.

Since completing his doctorate on Djuna Barnes, **Richard Espley** has published on Barnes and other modernists, the literary portrayal of London Zoo, commemorative representations of the First World War and issues of censorship in the modernism period. He has worked professionally in libraries for some years and is currently Head of Collections at Senate House Library, University of London.

David Grundy is a British Academy Postdoctoral Fellow at the University of Warwick, and the author of *A Black Arts Poetry Machine: Amiri Baraka and the Umbra Poets* (Bloomsbury, 2019). A poet and publisher, he co-runs the small press Materials and the magazine *Splinter*. He is currently working on a book entitled *Never By Itself Alone*, concerning queer poetics in Boston and San Francisco, and co-editing the forthcoming *Selected Poems of Calvin C. Hernton* (Wesleyan University Press).

Leila Kassir has worked in libraries for twenty years and is currently Academic Librarian for British, US, Latin American and Caribbean literature at Senate House Library. She is nearing the end of an MA by Research in English at Royal Holloway, University of London, researching the literary and archival representation of J. Lyons & Co. She has published on zines and fanzines and how libraries collect and use them.

Graham McKerrow is a journalist and political activist who edited leading gay and HIV/AIDS publications. He was involved in gay rights activism in Oxford in the 1970s, where he was also a representative on the Oxford Anti-Fascist Committee which organised opposition to the far-right National Front. He trained as a journalist on local newspapers and in 1980 he joined *Gay News* as a reporter and investigated police harassment and failings. The following year he co-founded and then co-edited *Capital Gay*, a campaigning weekly newspaper, which led coverage of HIV/AIDS as well as exposing police agents provocateurs and other harassment by the authorities, media, politicians and religious leaders. He was co-ordinator of the Defend Gay's the Word Campaign in the 1980s and in the 1990s edited the magazine *Positive Nation* for people with HIV/AIDS. He then spent 15 years at the *Guardian*, ultimately as editor of the *Guardian* and *Observer* Syndication Service.

Alexandra Parsons is a postdoctoral fellow at the Paul Mellon Centre for Studies in British Art and teaches literature and queer studies at Queen Mary, University of London. Her book, *Luminous Presence: Derek Jarman's Life-Writing*, is forthcoming from Manchester University Press.

Will Visconti completed a joint PhD in French Studies and Italian Studies at the University of Sydney. His teaching spans additional disciplines from history to modern languages at universities in Britain and Australia. From 2017 to 2018 he was a Visiting Fellow in the Institute of Modern Languages Research at Senate House, London. Since 2012 he has been involved with the Australasian Humour Studies Network and Centre for Media & Celebrity Studies. Visconti's research focuses on representations of gender, sexuality and transgression, particularly during the late nineteenth century. He is currently working on a biography of the performer Louise Weber, La Goulue.

Introduction: *Publishing Queer/Queer Publishing*

Leila Kassir and Richard Espley

From January to June 2018 the exhibition season *Queer Between the Covers* (QBTC) was held at Senate House Library, University of London. The season was based around a display of works from the library's collections showcasing a range of LGBTQ+ literature spanning over 300 years of publishing, with a corresponding series of events. The exhibition was subtitled *Literature, Queerness and the Library* and at its heart it aimed to examine the diverse ways in which literature has been central to cultural understanding of queerness, and how it has been used in equal measure to both educate and to celebrate, to mock and to denounce, with works by queer writers repeatedly read not only as art but as primary data on the nature of the LGBTQ+ experience. One of the overriding aims of the exhibition was to show how it has often been between the covers of books that struggles for acceptance, liberation and repression have been waged.

Concentrating on Senate House Library's own collections, the exhibition reflected how the library collected these works and with what emphases and omissions. What became evident as the exhibition developed was that the means of disseminating queer literature was at the heart of this story. Who published these works, how and where they were published, and for what audiences, provides an important social history of both expression and oppression, and one we decided to explore further with an exhibition-related conference entitled *Publishing Queer/Queer Publishing* which took place on 11 October 2018.

The call for papers suggested topics of focus including the evasion of censorship, criminal proceedings and the fear of them, histories of specific presses, cloaking and camouflage and the disguised queer story and alternative means of production and distribution such as underground presses. The ensuing conference was a lively and engaging event during which 12 papers were presented by researchers of queer book history both from within and outside of academia. One of the key aims of the conference and the entire season was to ensure participation from beyond the academy across a broad spectrum within the LGBTQ+ community (there is, of course, crossover). Five of the chapters in this book originated as papers at the *Publishing Queer/Queer Publishing* conference, while the chapter written by Graham McKerrow originated as a guest lecture given during the QBTC season.

One of the exhibits which formed part of the inspiration for the event was Djuna Barnes' *Ladies Almanack*, an extraordinary, bawdy exploration of a group of queer women. The book was published with great difficulty and bore false publisher information on the title page for fear of prosecution, and typified some of the issues we had suggested in the call for papers. However, while undeniably evasive, and characteristically so for Barnes, the book has also suffered from an over-identification with the Parisian salon of Natalie Clifford Barney; while clearly rooted in that community, the book's inventiveness and fantastical elements were lost as it became reduced to nothing more than a mildly salacious portrait of identifiable figures. Similarly, the book was for decades never mentioned without it being noted that Barnes had 'hawked' it around the streets of Paris, creating an impression of seedy erotica sold surreptitiously to tourists, while in truth Barnes had succeeded in selling dozens of hand-coloured copies for a remarkable $50. This idiosyncratic, densely allusive, witty and boldly experimental work which had struggled to find a place in a publishing market was then marginalised by decades of persistent categorical reduction, dismissed as either masked biography printed for a small coterie defined by a narrow view of their sexuality, or borderline pornography produced solely for financial gain.

One of the pleasures of working in a great library is the ability to put these fragments of history into the hands of others, and in this case the power and brio of the work are unmistakable, and so we brought a copy of Barnes' work in its first edition to the conference. Senate House Library is fortunate to also own a contemporary flyer that had been displayed in bookshops, undermining that image of Barnes stalking the boulevards with the entire print run under her cape. We left it on a table at the side of the room as a point of interest for speakers and delegates. As the day went on, not only did our speakers leave copies of items they were discussing alongside it, but we periodically visited the stacks to retrieve copies of other works being discussed. By the end of the day, we had an eclectic agglomeration of queer books which had chanced to be mentioned as forty people met in discussion; they were broadly bound by having queer authors, but not exclusively, and were drawn from different centuries and languages. As they were cleared away, we couldn't help but reflect on the shifting and contingent nature of the portrait of queer culture they represented; while an accurate reflection of a day's discussion, they were by no means a queer canon, nor is it conceivable that should another conference be organised, exactly the same works would be fetched.

This partial selection irresistibly drew to mind the events which Graham McKerrow so powerfully describes in his chapter. Operation Tiger, where ʰish Customs and Excise raided Gay's the Word bookshop to seek out ᵊnce of obscenity amongst imported books, had hung over the entire ⁺ion season, and the conference. While the list of books confiscated was almost comically inept (the confiscation of Christine de Pizan standing out), it had been clear to us as librarians that the vast majority of the titles had been sitting on the shelves of Senate House Library at the s ame time, frequently in the same editions. Their claimed obscenity, and their queerness, manifested itself to officials in their being gathered together in Bloomsbury in a queer space, from which they then chose their own partial and inadequate selection for their own pseudo-judicial and punitive purposes. As we filled trolleys with our own selection at the end of the conference, there was an almost comical mirroring, as two groups, faced with a vast body of literature, had haphazardly amassed two selections that seemed to them obscurely to be genuinely or meaningfully queer.

At first that thought raised a wry smile, but on reflection it does speak loudly to the role of community and communities here, and how publishing interacts with the very idea of queer identities. These contingent, nourishing groupings recall what McKerrow describes as the 'eco-system of cooperation and exchange' which underpinned the community around Gay's the Word bookshop, and was essential during their struggles against Customs and Excise. Indeed, those books could be viewed as fulfilling the same supportive function, or as inspiring forebears, rather as Alexandra Parsons explores in her chapter. Parsons quotes Derek Jarman reflecting on his student days at King's College London as he 'began to read between the lines of history. The hunt was on for forebears who validated' his existence. Jarman's comment about the importance of books in the understanding of queer identities corresponds with the impetus for our conference's focus on publishing books that are both explicitly queer or, as Jarman described, the queer narrative emerged from a close reading.

Many of the chapters published here echo themes of collaboration and adaptation which, in varied forms, permeate through the works and publishing processes under consideration and reflect an important aspect of queer literature and publishing. The necessity of cooperation, either to ensure survival through strength in numbers or emotional connection, is reflected in the community-oriented works of Valerie Taylor, the subject of Jennifer Dentel's chapter. Taylor would feature details of Chicago's queer spaces in her novels, thus providing her readers with a ready-made, but discreetly published, map to a potential supportive network. Marketed for titillation, these works could therefore fulfil a redemptive purpose for a hidden community of readers.

Many of the works under consideration feature creative collaborations, including the dual-city publication of the probably multi-authored *Teleny*, the history of which is elaborated in Will Visconti's chapter. For all of the considerable discussion of its creation, Visconti finds a collaborative community in its group of authors. Intriguingly, he also sees in the book's structural instability and its frequent reaching out to other texts not only a community but a manifestation of the unease and uncertain status of its potential readership.

The exchange of information is sometimes reworked into adaptation of existing works, either by re-editing self-created works or by incorporating and collaging works from other sources, or in some cases via both methods. Book artist Jeremy Dixon describes his artistic process, incorporating found items in his print storytelling, while John Wieners, the poet at the heart of David Grundy's chapter, was involved with the countercultural magazine *Fag Rag*, which regularly included radical reuse and collage. The process underlying Derek Jarman's reinterpretation of his film *Caravaggio* into a published form is explored by Alexandra Parsons.

However, there is a limit to the extent to which such collaboration and such community can be presented purely as a redemptive force, and sometimes it is a mark of a struggle for any self-expression in the face of overwhelming odds. David Grundy powerfully describes John Wieners' battles with his typesetters and the violent censorship and suppression of his body and mind whilst in state hospitals, and the impact these forces had on his innovative publishing practice.

Such repression recalls comments made by a delegate on the day of the conference, on the meaning and validity of the word 'activism' in this context, a word which recurred throughout the day to describe submerged and overt struggles for a voice. A tenet of the *Queer Between the Covers* season was that suppression or destruction of books was often a proxy for threatened or imagined violence towards queer bodies and lives, but we had a sobering and important discussion on the nature of the challenges which present themselves, and whether 'activism' in the context of publishing is a justifiable term set against those queer figures campaigning and falling victim to open brutality, imprisonment, institutionalisation or murder.

One community which is markedly absent here is representation from or discussion of trans and trans+ contributions to publishing, or intersection with publishing forms. In a collection this small, there are of course many absences, but this one was felt particularly keenly. We would like to record our regret that a contribution from Charles Ledbetter had to be withdrawn for reasons beyond all of our control. Charles' paper and subsequent essay looked at the possibility of trans publishing as a subversive material practice, using a case study of Immanion Press, a small press whose main activity is the publication of speculative fiction foregrounding trans subject matter. We have lost an engaging and important piece on the analysis and subversion of hierarchical power relationships between publishers, authors and readers here, and we hope our readers will encounter it in another publication in due course.

As editors, we would also recognise the whiteness of the contributions both in content and authorship, something we profoundly regret, but something we want to foreground. We continue to discuss within the Library and across the University strategies to obviate a bias seen across academia, not least to work harder to diversify the channels through which we distribute calls for papers. We are also committed to introducing anonymised gathering of data on how all prospective speakers would describe their background for future conferences, as in a world of remote contact we were unaware of the whiteness of our cohort until the day of the event itself.

We are, however, delighted to be able to offer this one contingent selection of contributions to a vast conversation which is undyingly rich in its challenges and its opportunities to uplift and support, and to nourish multiple and multiplying, shifting communities. We would be delighted to see it play a small role in shaping that ongoing discussion, and perhaps helping to embed the histories of publishing more directly into the twin histories of direct homophobia, suffering and death on one hand and the love and joy of queer lives on the other.

1. 'A gay presence': publication and revision in John Wieners' *Behind the State Capitol*[1]

David Grundy

John Wieners' life and work is often framed within the 'New American Poetry' and attendant literary communities. Yet though he appeared in Donald Allen's influential 1959 anthology, and was friends with major figures among the groups famously named in it, he is often painted as something of a tragic outlier: his experiences with drug addiction, mental illness and homophobia rendered him *poète maudite* or 'outsider artist', a supreme poet of loneliness, cut off from social sustenance.

As I aim to demonstrate, this narrative is inadequate, particularly when Wieners' work of the 1970s is considered, produced within the orbit of the little-studied, Boston-based activist collectives *Fag Rag* and the Good Gay Poets. Working-class, politically radical and containing early manifestations of 'genderfuck', these currents offered an alternative to the dark side of identity politics and the internalised homophobia and transphobia they perpetuated. Good Gay Poets published Wieners' *Behind the State Capitol: or Cincinnati Pike* in 1975, and it's my contention that this much-misunderstood book is a crucial document in the history of gender non-conformity, and present trans and non-binary rights movements, as they emerged from within the class and gender bifurcations of early Gay Liberation Movement activism. Focusing on the importance of publication contexts and revisions to Wieners' work, this chapter thus seeks to restore what has hitherto remained a cult classic to its rightful place at the centre of American queer writing.

Since his emergence into the late 1950s literary scene, Wieners had published hundreds of poems in little magazines, but only a handful of full-length collections. So in December 1975, when *State Capitol* was published, ̶ ̶ns were high: released in a hardback edition of 100 and a paperback

̶le to Wieners' 1972 pamphlet *Playboy* (*We Were There: A ̶*
̶onvention*) (Boston, MA: Good Gay Poets). I gra̶
Academy postdoctoral early career fello̶
̶o Michael Bronski, Raymond Foye and M̶
̶eviewers for their helpful comments. T̶
̶nich had a crucial impact on some o̶

̶n and revision in John Wieners' *Beh̶*
̶ween the Covers: Histories of Queer ̶*
̶ondon Press, 2021), pp. 7–31. Licen̶

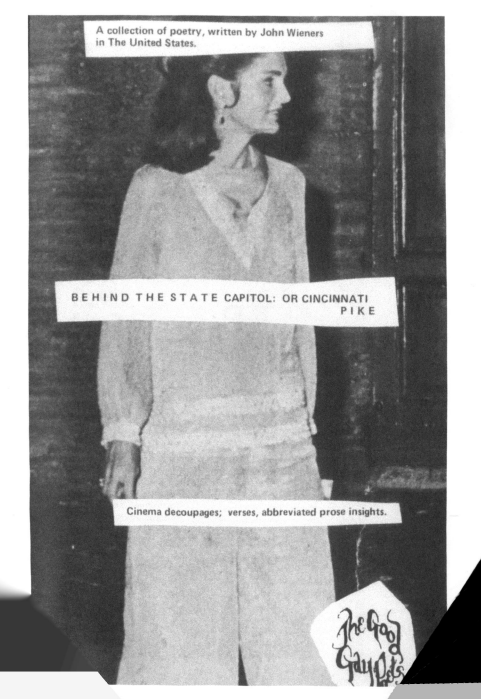

A collection of poetry, written by John Wieners in The United States.

BEHIND THE STATE CAPITOL: OR CINCINNATI PIKE

Cinema decoupages; verses, abbreviated prose insights.

The Good Gay Poets

...he State Capitol: or Cincinnati Pike *by John Wieners.* ...
...oye, Wieners' literary executor.

of 1500, each numbering some 204 pages, the book collected together much of the highly prolific Wieners' poetry from the previous six years and was his longest publication to date. Wieners' last full-length book, the 1972 *Selected Poems*, had been primarily retrospective, and the new volume promised to update readers on what had been a productive first half of the new, post-Stonewall decade. Yet *State Capitol* would prove to be in some ways 'both the capstone of Wieners' career and the book that would sink his reputation'.[2] Receiving little notice at the time, the book's failure saw Wieners essentially disappear from public life. Though he continued to write in private, Wieners published little and gave few public readings after around 1976, famously claiming, 'I am living out the logical conclusion of my books'.[3]

According to Jim Dunn, 'When [*State Capitol*] was published in 1975, the silence and lack of response [...] was deafening. Of the few reviews the book received, two of them were by writers involved with the printing and publishing of the book [Charley Shively and Alan Davies]'.[4] As well as much new work, *State Capitol* contained revised versions of poems that had appeared in magazines throughout the 1960s and early 1970s. Yet Wieners was not interested in preserving, collecting or reproducing. The book is subtitled 'Cinema decoupages; verses, abbreviated prose insights': earlier poems are treated as material to be collaged and revised alongside newer, more experimental material, challenging Wieners' reputation as a writer of standalone lyric poems in favour of a tonally broad, gender-fluid and generically unstable poetics. For George Butterick, the revisions to previously published work were 'in almost every case [...] for the poorer'. They eliminate 'the spoken directness and accuracy of the original'. These changes 'are simply strange if not inept', he continues, 'and they are endemic throughout the volume. The poet has forsaken his own genius and the stark simplicity of the original statements, so forthright they cannot be doubted or denied'.[5] Wieners' friend Robert Duncan, who'd favourably reviewed *Ace of Pentacles* a decade previously, was apparently incensed, believing that the Good Gay Poets were trying to destroy Wieners' reputation. Likewise, William Corbett, with whom Wieners, Lee Harwood and Lewis Warsh had edited *The Boston Eagle* magazine, felt that 'something had happened' to the lyric poet of *Ace of Pentacles*, *Nerves* and *Asylum Poems*, and that the book was 'a record of

2   Geoff Ward, *The Writing of America: Literature and Cultural Identity from the Puritans to the Present* (Cambridge: Polity Press, 2002), 92.

3   Raymond Foye, 'A visit with John Wieners' (1984), in John Wieners, *Cultural Affairs in Boston: Poetry and Prose 1956–1985* (Santa Barbara, CA: Black Sparrow Press, 1988), 17 (henceforth *CAIB*).

4   Jim Dunn, *The Mesmerizing Apparition of the Oracle of Joy Street: A Critical Study of John Wieners' Life and Later Work in Boston*. Master's thesis, Harvard Extension School. Online <http://nrs.harvard.edu/urn-3:HUL.InstRepos:33826277>, 3–4. Dunn here refers to Charley Shively, 'What happened to the mind of John Wieners?' [rev. of *Behind the State Capitol*], *Gay Sunshine* 32: 27–8, spring 1977; and Alan Davies, 'An hardness prompts literature', *Poetry Project Newsletter*, 1976, repr. in *Mirage: John Wieners Issue*, 30–7, 1985.

5   Quoted in Dunn, *Mesmerizing Apparition*, 37.

Figure 1.2. Frontispiece from Behind the State Capitol: or Cincinnati Pike by John Wieners. Permission granted by Raymond Foye, Wieners' literary executor.

disintegration'.[6] Though contemporary critics ostensibly praise the book, misinformation still spreads: that it was 'famously, typeset from [Wieners'] drafts with nearly no editorial correction', and that its 'typos, irregular stanza formation' and 'interminable sentences that do not parse' are 'the epitome of a form of "outsider writing"'.[7]

As I will show, the actual process of production was far more collaborative than this characterisation suggests. Wieners actively embraced error as a key principle of his poetics, and rather than placing Wieners' work within the problematic lineage of 'outsider' writing, it's this work's relation to *community* that I want to emphasise here: from the young, queer Boston poets of the 1950s and 1960s (Wieners, Stephen Jonas, Ed Marshall and others) whom Gerrit Lansing called the 'occult school of Boston', to the emergence in the 1970s of gay *Fag Rag* and of younger writers and activists, such as Charley Shively, who idolised Wieners as a pioneering queer voice of earlier decades, currently producing his queerest and most formally experimental material. Without losing one's sense of its sheer strangeness, *State Capitol* is best read as a work that emerged from and in dialogue with a (number of) queer social context(s), as well as a groundbreaking influence on queer writing to come, perhaps most notably the predominantly San Francisco-based New Narrative writers, many of whom idolised Wieners and paid tribute to him throughout their work.[8]

Given this, viewing *Behind the State Capitol* through the lens of publication history and revision serves as a contextual corrective and suggests how the text might be read anew through a queer lens. The term 'revision' should here be understood not only in terms of revisions to existing poems (the target of Butterick's critique), but in Wieners' understanding of poetic language itself as a constant process of collage, revision and performance. I'll begin by setting the book's publication in the context of Wieners' friendship with Shively and participation in the *Fag Rag* collective in the early 1970s. The chapter will then discuss Wieners' gender identifications and textual performances as forms of revision in themselves, contrasting Wieners' queer, 'genderfuck' personas with subsequent critical misreadings. It will conclude with an examination of Wieners' status as a psychiatric survivor, resituating questions of revision and publication in the context of mental health institutions and the web of homophobia, classism and neurotypical violence which tried to silence Wieners' poetic voice(s).

6   Quoted in Dunn, *Mesmerizing Apparition*, 43. Corbett later revised his opinion: see 'William Corbett: "Charity Balls" by John Wieners'. Video footage from *A Legacy Celebration of John Wieners*, St Mark's Poetry Project, 6 Apr. 2016. Online <https://www.youtube.com/watch?v=q3-UOrQilM0>.

7   Brian Kim Stefans, *Word Toys: Poetry and Technics* (Tuscaloosa, AL: University of Alabama Press, 2017), 131.

8   See, in particular, *Mirage: John Wieners Issue*, ed. Kevin Killian (1985).

Olson, poet of the
Poems and Professor of *???*
here, John Wieners, author of
the **Hotel Wentley Poems** and
Ace of Pentacles and Ed Sanders, editor of **F??k You: A Magazine of The Arts,** and author of
Peace Eye (including the 'Gobble
Gang' poems) read their poetry to
an appreciative audience in what
could be viewed as an precursor
to the Berkeley Poetry Conference in Berkeley California,
last summer Culminating in that
Conference, last year seemed,
among other things, to be the
'Year of the Poet'

   Mr Olson had read some new
work; Mr. Wieners read from
the **Ace of Pentacles;** Mr Sanders read from **Poem from Jail**
and the 'Gobble Gang' the reading was 'just right'

   Buffalo had become through
the previous two years the sort
of 'open' society for modern
poetry (in the tradition of Olson,
not Merwin) rather than a 'closed' group, such as those of the
San Francisco poets, or the Low-
er East Side. At the beginning
the attraction was, of course,
Charles Olson, former rector of
the experimental Black Mountain College in the mid 50's and
sort of 'father' of the school of
poets from 1950 and on.

Clues To Character

Jones, Robert Kelly and others
teaching courses and giving readings. Mr. Weiners came the following winter Then came the
Spring Arts Festival of 1965 and
the Berkeley Conference of the
summer

   At Berkley virtually all the
modern poets were present with a
few notable exceptions. Even
though the Conference had a ten-
dency to be dominated by the
San Francisco group, and suffered from semi-incompetent
planning, the Conference was a
success. Its timing was perfect
in the view of the past decade
and a ha *?? ???*

179

Figure 1.3. p. 179 from Behind the State Capitol: or Cincinnati Pike *by John Wieners.*
Permission granted by Raymond Foye, Wieners' literary executor.

'New love, encountered between strangers': Wieners and *Fag Rag* in the 1970s

Following the appearance of the foundational, openly queer *Hotel Wentley Poems* in 1958, Wieners had undergone a troubled 1960s. Repeatedly institutionalised, often at the behest of his parents, who were alarmed by their son's gender non-conforming behaviour and bohemian lifestyle, he suffered the debilitating effects of intensive recreational drug use and the 'treatments' he received in asylums. This might be electroshock 'therapy' or heavy and debilitating doses of pharmaceuticals ('in early morning / insulin comas, convulsions, fifty-one thousand injections', as one poem has it).[9] Wieners was sustained through such traumatic experiences by a community of queer fellow writers and friends who, like him, have often fallen through the cracks of mainstream literary history and even alternative canon-building. Charles Olson's influence on Wieners' earlier work has often been remarked: less noted is the sustaining atmosphere of the Boston 'Occult School' and its San Francisco accomplices. A key document here is the *Boston Newsletter* of 1956, put together by Wieners, Joe Dunn, Jack Spicer, Robin Blaser and Stephen Jonas with instructions to 'post whatever pages of it poke you in the eye in the most public place you can find – i.e. an art gallery, a bohemian bar, or a lavatory frequented by poets.'[10]

Outside of Boston, Wieners also maintained important friendships with other gay poets such as Frank O'Hara, Allen Ginsberg and Michael Rumaker, and was open about his sexuality with bi- or heterosexual poets like Amiri Baraka or Ed Dorn, establishing himself as a key figure in the New American Poetry and spending time in New York and at SUNY Buffalo. Despite his travels, Wieners was very much a Boston poet, his work attesting to the queer subculture and sharp class divisions that marked the city and to what Maria Damon calls 'the matrix of Massachusetts institutions' from the Charles Street Jail to Taunton State Hospital and the titular State Capitol, the State's seat of government.[11] While interned in Central Islip State Hospital following a 1969 arrest on a forgery charge in New York, Wieners received a letter from the poet Charley Shively. Establishing a tone of respectful flirtation, Shively impressed ~~o~~lder Wieners with his knowledge of his poetry and Wieners relished the ~~~~ with a younger representative of a newly flourishing queer, activist ~~~~ his isolation in the academic enclaves of Buffalo, writing 'I am ~~~~ eyes, 12 teeth left, bad eyesight, etc. Your life sounds ~~~~ friendship.'[12] The correspondence began concurrent~~l~~

~~~~ depts. of the treasury. *Secret Service* duration~~~~
~~~~ oets, 1975) (henceforth *BTSC*), 98.
~~~~ er papers, Stuart A. Rose Manuscript
~~~~ eartfelt thanks to the late Kevin Killi~~~~
~~~~ arm for the original discovery.
~~~~ in the matrix of Massachus~~~~
of *Beat Studies*, 3: 69–92, 2014.
*Voices': The Letters of John Wiene~~r~~

with the Stonewall Uprising: Shively, four years younger than Wieners and a professor at Boston State College, was also an anarchist and an early pioneer of the Boston gay rights movement. Upon his release, Shively took Wieners to meetings and social events of the Boston Student Homophile League, introducing him to a new circle of younger queer activists which rejuvenated his work.[13]

Through such friendships, Wieners found himself part of a new, post-Stonewall surge of gay publishing and activism in Boston, whose radical critique of American society and its institutions had been suggested in the bohemian circles of 1960s American poetry, but was now given an internationalist and intersectional orientation within an explicitly queer context. Though there could be gendered tensions between gays and lesbians, and the whiteness of the Gay Liberation Movement received criticism, links were being drawn between older gay male traditions and emerging intersectional politics of Third-Worldism and feminism to expressions of queer, trans and 'genderfuck' identity.[14] In 1971, a group including Shively, Wieners, Michael Bronski and John Mitzel formed the Boston gay newsletter *Fag Rag*. With Shively at the centre, the collective was run on an anarchist, cooperative basis, with a core of members, as well as visiting or occasional participants. It was in Boston that the Combahee River Collective was formed in 1974 by a group of Black lesbian feminists who would play vital roles in the development of a new politics focused on the hitherto neglected role of queer women of colour, and the *Fag Rag* collective shared offices at 22 Bromfield Street with *Gay Community News*, members of whom were also involved with the Combahee Collective.[15] Mirroring the publishing processes of the Women's and Black Arts Movements, *Fag Rag* was part of a nationwide network of papers in Detroit, San Francisco and New York. Brightly coloured and militant in both its politics and aesthetics, the magazine featured essays, letters, activist reports, poems and visual art which often bordered on the pornographic. Seen as too trashy and working class for some – Susan Sontag apparently said that the magazine needed to reach a broader audience – *Fag Rag* was at one point described by New Hampshire governor Meldrim Thomson as 'the most loathsome publication in the English language'.[16] But Wieners – listed as a collective member in some issues, though his exact contribution is unclear – revelled in appearing in such

Works. Online <https://academicworks.cuny.edu/gc_etds/292> (456).

Stewart, 'For the Voices', 490–1.

e.g., Allen Young, 'Gay women and men: how we relate', *Gay Sunshine* 21: 8–9, s

Christopher Lonc, 'Genderfuck and its delights', *Gay Sunshine* 21: 4–16, sprin

Shively, 'Fag Rag: the most loathsome publication in the English language',

the Vietnam Era Underground Press, Part 2, ed. Ken Wachsberger (Ann

iversity Press, 2012).

'Sequins and switchblades: in extremis exegesis. A reading of

'58–1984', *Fag Rag* 44: 28–33 (29), 1984.

012.

company, his poems, essays and other unclassifiable texts frequently appearing under the name Jacqueline Wieners.

In 1972, members of the *Fag Rag* group, again with Shively at the centre, started the Good Gay Poets, the name a pun on Walt Whitman's famous designation as the 'Good Gray Poet'.[17] Their second publication was Wieners' joyous poem 'Playboy', recording the visit made by members of the *Fag Rag* collective to the 1972 Democratic Convention in Miami and delineating the new context Wieners had found. 'I delight in sharing group feeling. / Evening vigils, drag queens, movie actors, marijuana', he writes, linking this socialised vision of love to the personal and social love of the 1950s: 'New love, encountered between strangers / maybe or it's old love come back.'[18]

Typesetting, labour and queer collaboration

Such contexts gave Wieners' work a new political charge, as his poems began to articulate a class-conscious, psychiatric survivor identity suggesting the need for revolutionary change.[19] But the queer politics of this work also operate in terms of form, when it is at its most obtuse, as well as when it is direct. Around 1969, Wieners had begun experimenting with form, typography and voicing in ways not seen in his work since his earliest, generally unpublished poems.[20] Raymond Foye, who would go on to edit Wieners' next two books, noted in 1984:

> [H]e's after a reductive, abbreviated expression ... If a typo creeps in, he insists it stay. If I mistakenly break a line while typing up a new poem, that must stay, too. If I can't decipher a word & ask him what it is, he looks into the aether and pulls down a word that is as much of a non sequitur as possible. It's all an open-ended flux.[21]

Wieners worked closely with Charley Shively on *Behind the State Capitol*, a process Shively later documented in the essay 'JohnJob', published in the 1985 Wieners issue of the magazine *Mirage*.[22] As Shively notes, when Good

---

17 Shively, '*Fag Rag* ...', lists the original group as including 'Aaron Shurin, Ron Schreiber, myself, David Eberly, Charles River, and John LaPorta', to which Michael Bronski adds Sal Farinella, Walta Borawski, Rudy Kikel and David Emerson Smith (author's interview with Michael Bronski, London, Dec. 2019).

18 *CAIB*, 124.

19 *SP*, 17–18.

20 For this early poetry, see the eight uncollected poems in *Floating Bear*, 10, 1961; 'A Proposition' (unpublished poem, May 1957), in *Letters, with Poems, to Michael Rumaker, 1955–1958*, *Battersea Review*, online <http://thebatterseareview.com/critical-prose/218-letters-with-poems-to-michael-rumaker-1955-58>; and 'End chapters in autobiography' and 'The bridge word', *Chicago Review*, 12 (1), spring 1958.

21 Quoted in Andrea Brady, '"Making use of this pain": the John Wieners Archive', *Paideuma* 36 (1–2): 131–79, 2007–9.

22 Charley Shively, 'JohnJob: editing *Behind the State Capitol or Cincinnati Pike*', *Mirage: John Wieners Issue*, 78–82, 1985.

Gay Poets published *State Capitol*, 'the work signalled an emerging energy and possibility of gay publishing, which had yet to be realised'. Despite the appearance of gay poetry anthologies such as Winston Leyland's 1975 *Angels of the Lyre*, large-scale collections of explicitly queer poetry like Wieners' were few and far between. As Shively writes, 'in 1974 & 75 we were only beginning to create our own medium'.[23] Wieners could have published with more established presses, and would later publish two full-length, career-spanning books with Black Sparrow. But, as Shively suggests, after the manuscript was turned down by Jonathan Cape, who'd published his previous *Selected Poems*, Wieners 'looked to the Good Gay Poets because it was not established, because it represented a coming to flower of newly released and previously unrehearsed energies.'[24]

Inspired by underground publications of the 1960s mimeo revolution like Ed Sanders' *Fuck You: A Magazine of the Arts*, a complete run of which Wieners gave to Shively as inspiration, Shively saw *Fag Rag* and the Good Gay Poets as a way to 'bring total freedom to authors, allowing each of us to write whatever and however we wished. What we needed most was not respect from the straight world but respect for each other's work.'[25] This goes completely against accounts that saw *State Capitol* as an embarrassing example of mental disintegration – which included not only those of Black Sparrow publisher John Martin, with its veiled homophobia, but of Wieners' friend and queer poetic colleague Robert Duncan.[26] Wieners *wanted* his work to appear this way.

State Capitol emerged in close collaboration with the publishers, its juxtaposition of lyric poetry, multiple voices, queer collages, class consciousness, gossip and high camp and – in particular – its visual appearance clearly reflecting the *Fag Rag* aesthetic. The 'cinema decoupages' of the book's subtitle refer both to the book's collages – collaborations between Wieners, Shively and John Mitzel – and to the poems in which words, letters and phrases are 'cut out', creating new juxtapositions and ambiguities. Wieners had worked on the manuscript for some years with an intern from Boston College: 'hacking, stuffing and reshelving' rather than making 'improvements'. This process of revising earlier, previously published texts reflected Wieners' general practice for years afterwards of annotating and decoupaging his own copies of his published books, from which he would improvise at public readings (Shively notes Wieners reading in this way at St Mark's Poetry Project as early as 1968). The cheapness of the book's design, resulting from the relative lack of resources for a grassroots publisher, happily merged with Wieners' own aesthetic practice and with the collective, collaborative nature of its publication.

23   Shively, 'JohnJob', 78.
24   Ibid.
25   Ibid.
26   Dunn, *Mesmerizing Apparition*, 43.

1. 'A gay presence': publication and revision in John Wieners' *Behind the State Capitol*[1]

David Grundy

John Wieners' life and work is often framed within the 'New American Poetry' and attendant literary communities. Yet though he appeared in Donald Allen's influential 1959 anthology, and was friends with major figures among the groups famously named in it, he is often painted as something of a tragic outlier: his experiences with drug addiction, mental illness and homophobia rendered him *poète maudite* or 'outsider artist', a supreme poet of loneliness, cut off from social sustenance.

As I aim to demonstrate, this narrative is inadequate, particularly when Wieners' work of the 1970s is considered, produced within the orbit of the little-studied, Boston-based activist collectives *Fag Rag* and the Good Gay Poets. Working-class, politically radical and containing early manifestations of 'genderfuck', these currents offered an alternative to the dark side of identity politics and the internalised homophobia and transphobia they perpetuated. Good Gay Poets published Wieners' *Behind the State Capitol: or Cincinnati Pike* in 1975, and it's my contention that this much-misunderstood book is a crucial document in the history of gender non-conformity, and present trans and non-binary rights movements, as they emerged from within the class and gender bifurcations of early Gay Liberation Movement activism. Focusing on the importance of publication contexts and revisions to Wieners' work, this chapter thus seeks to restore what has hitherto remained a cult classic to its rightful place at the centre of American queer writing.

Since his emergence into the late 1950s literary scene, Wieners had published hundreds of poems in little magazines, but only a handful of full-length collections. So in December 1975, when *State Capitol* was published, expectations were high: released in a hardback edition of 100 and a paperback

1   'A Gay Presence' is the subtitle to Wieners' 1972 pamphlet *Playboy* (*We Were There: A Gay Presence at the Miami Democratic Convention*) (Boston, MA: Good Gay Poets). I gratefully acknowledge the support of a British Academy postdoctoral early career fellowship in conducting this research. Many thanks to Michael Bronski, Raymond Foye and Michael Seth Stewart and to the anonymous peer reviewers for their helpful comments. Thanks also to Nat Raha for sharing critical work which had a crucial impact on some of the ideas here discussed.

Figure 1.1. Behind the State Capitol: or Cincinnati Pike *by John Wieners. Permission granted by Raymond Foye, Wieners' literary executor.*

of 1500, each numbering some 204 pages, the book collected together much of the highly prolific Wieners' poetry from the previous six years and was his longest publication to date. Wieners' last full-length book, the 1972 *Selected Poems*, had been primarily retrospective, and the new volume promised to update readers on what had been a productive first half of the new, post-Stonewall decade. Yet *State Capitol* would prove to be in some ways 'both the capstone of Wieners' career and the book that would sink his reputation'.[2] Receiving little notice at the time, the book's failure saw Wieners essentially disappear from public life. Though he continued to write in private, Wieners published little and gave few public readings after around 1976, famously claiming, 'I am living out the logical conclusion of my books'.[3]

According to Jim Dunn, 'When [*State Capitol*] was published in 1975, the silence and lack of response [...] was deafening. Of the few reviews the book received, two of them were by writers involved with the printing and publishing of the book [Charley Shively and Alan Davies]'.[4] As well as much new work, *State Capitol* contained revised versions of poems that had appeared in magazines throughout the 1960s and early 1970s. Yet Wieners was not interested in preserving, collecting or reproducing. The book is subtitled 'Cinema decoupages; verses, abbreviated prose insights': earlier poems are treated as material to be collaged and revised alongside newer, more experimental material, challenging Wieners' reputation as a writer of standalone lyric poems in favour of a tonally broad, gender-fluid and generically unstable poetics. For George Butterick, the revisions to previously published work were 'in almost every case [...] for the poorer'. They eliminate 'the spoken directness and accuracy of the original'. These changes 'are simply strange if not inept', he continues, 'and they are endemic throughout the volume. The poet has forsaken his own genius and the stark simplicity of the original statements, so forthright they cannot be doubted or denied'.[5] Wieners' friend Robert Duncan, who'd favourably reviewed *Ace of Pentacles* a decade previously, was apparently incensed, believing that the Good Gay Poets were trying to destroy Wieners' reputation. Likewise, William Corbett, with whom Wieners, Lee Harwood and Lewis Warsh had edited *The Boston Eagle* magazine, felt that 'something had happened' to the lyric poet of *Ace of Pentacles*, *Nerves* and *Asylum Poems*, and that the book was 'a record of

2   Geoff Ward, *The Writing of America: Literature and Cultural Identity from the Puritans to the Present* (Cambridge: Polity Press, 2002), 92.

3   Raymond Foye, 'A visit with John Wieners' (1984), in John Wieners, *Cultural Affairs in Boston: Poetry and Prose 1956–1985* (Santa Barbara, CA: Black Sparrow Press, 1988), 17 (henceforth *CAIB*).

4   Jim Dunn, *The Mesmerizing Apparition of the Oracle of Joy Street: A Critical Study of John Wieners' Life and Later Work in Boston*. Master's thesis, Harvard Extension School. Online <http://nrs.harvard.edu/urn-3:HUL.InstRepos:33826277>, 3–4. Dunn here refers to Charley Shively, 'What happened to the mind of John Wieners?' [rev. of *Behind the State Capitol*], *Gay Sunshine* 32: 27–8, spring 1977; and Alan Davies, 'An hardness prompts literature', *Poetry Project Newsletter*, 1976, repr. in *Mirage: John Wieners Issue*, 30–7, 1985.

5   Quoted in Dunn, *Mesmerizing Apparition*, 37.

Figure 1.2. Frontispiece from Behind the State Capitol: or Cincinnati Pike by John
Wieners. Permission granted by Raymond Foye, Wieners' literary executor.

disintegration'.[6] Though contemporary critics ostensibly praise the book, misinformation still spreads: that it was 'famously, typeset from [Wieners'] drafts with nearly no editorial correction', and that its 'typos, irregular stanza formation' and 'interminable sentences that do not parse' are 'the epitome of a form of "outsider writing"'.[7]

As I will show, the actual process of production was far more collaborative than this characterisation suggests. Wieners actively embraced error as a key principle of his poetics, and rather than placing Wieners' work within the problematic lineage of 'outsider' writing, it's this work's relation to *community* that I want to emphasise here: from the young, queer Boston poets of the 1950s and 1960s (Wieners, Stephen Jonas, Ed Marshall and others) whom Gerrit Lansing called the 'occult school of Boston', to the emergence in the 1970s of gay *Fag Rag* and of younger writers and activists, such as Charley Shively, who idolised Wieners as a pioneering queer voice of earlier decades, currently producing his queerest and most formally experimental material. Without losing one's sense of its sheer strangeness, *State Capitol* is best read as a work that emerged from and in dialogue with a (number of) queer social context(s), as well as a groundbreaking influence on queer writing to come, perhaps most notably the predominantly San Francisco-based New Narrative writers, many of whom idolised Wieners and paid tribute to him throughout their work.[8]

Given this, viewing *Behind the State Capitol* through the lens of publication history and revision serves as a contextual corrective and suggests how the text might be read anew through a queer lens. The term 'revision' should here be understood not only in terms of revisions to existing poems (the target of Butterick's critique), but in Wieners' understanding of poetic language itself as a constant process of collage, revision and performance. I'll begin by setting the book's publication in the context of Wieners' friendship with Shively and participation in the *Fag Rag* collective in the early 1970s. The chapter will then discuss Wieners' gender identifications and textual performances as forms of revision in themselves, contrasting Wieners' queer, 'genderfuck' personas with subsequent critical misreadings. It will conclude with an examination of Wieners' status as a psychiatric survivor, resituating questions of revision and publication in the context of mental health institutions and the web of homophobia, classism and neurotypical violence which tried to silence Wieners' poetic voice(s).

6   Quoted in Dunn, *Mesmerizing Apparition*, 43. Corbett later revised his opinion: see 'William Corbett: "Charity Balls" by John Wieners'. Video footage from *A Legacy Celebration of John Wieners*, St Mark's Poetry Project, 6 Apr. 2016. Online <https://www.youtube.com/watch?v=q3-UOrQiIM0>.

7   Brian Kim Stefans, *Word Toys: Poetry and Technics* (Tuscaloosa, AL: University of Alabama Press, 2017), 131.

8   See, in particular, *Mirage: John Wieners Issue*, ed. Kevin Killian (1985).

Figure 1.3. p. 179 from Behind the State Capitol: or Cincinnati Pike *by John Wieners. Permission granted by Raymond Foye, Wieners' literary executor.*

'New love, encountered between strangers': Wieners and *Fag Rag* in the 1970s

Following the appearance of the foundational, openly queer *Hotel Wentley Poems* in 1958, Wieners had undergone a troubled 1960s. Repeatedly institutionalised, often at the behest of his parents, who were alarmed by their son's gender non-conforming behaviour and bohemian lifestyle, he suffered the debilitating effects of intensive recreational drug use and the 'treatments' he received in asylums. This might be electroshock 'therapy' or heavy and debilitating doses of pharmaceuticals ('in early morning / insulin comas, convulsions, fifty-one thousand injections', as one poem has it).[9] Wieners was sustained through such traumatic experiences by a community of queer fellow writers and friends who, like him, have often fallen through the cracks of mainstream literary history and even alternative canon-building. Charles Olson's influence on Wieners' earlier work has often been remarked: less noted is the sustaining atmosphere of the Boston 'Occult School' and its San Francisco accomplices. A key document here is the *Boston Newsletter* of 1956, put together by Wieners, Joe Dunn, Jack Spicer, Robin Blaser and Stephen Jonas with instructions to 'post whatever pages of it poke you in the eye in the most public place you can find – i.e. an art gallery, a bohemian bar, or a lavatory frequented by poets.'[10]

Outside of Boston, Wieners also maintained important friendships with other gay poets such as Frank O'Hara, Allen Ginsberg and Michael Rumaker, and was open about his sexuality with bi- or heterosexual poets like Amiri Baraka or Ed Dorn, establishing himself as a key figure in the New American Poetry and spending time in New York and at SUNY Buffalo. Despite his travels, Wieners was very much a Boston poet, his work attesting to the queer subculture and sharp class divisions that marked the city and to what Maria Damon calls 'the matrix of Massachusetts institutions' from the Charles Street Jail to Taunton State Hospital and the titular State Capitol, the State's seat of government.[11] While interned in Central Islip State Hospital following a 1969 arrest on a forgery charge in New York, Wieners received a letter from the poet Charley Shively. Establishing a tone of respectful flirtation, Shively impressed the older Wieners with his knowledge of his poetry and Wieners relished the encounter with a younger representative of a newly flourishing queer, activist sociality after his isolation in the academic enclaves of Buffalo, writing 'I am 5'9" and some, blue eyes, 12 teeth left, bad eyesight, etc. Your life sounds fruitful enough for a friendship.'[12] The correspondence began concurrently

---

9   'To the bad debts in the *United States* depts. of the treasury. *Secret Service* duration', *Behind the State Capitol* (Boston, MA: Good Gay Poets, 1975) (henceforth *BTSC*), 98.

10   *Boston Newsletter* (carbon copy, Jack Spicer papers, Stuart A. Rose Manuscript, Archives and Rare Book Library, Emory University). Heartfelt thanks to the late Kevin Killian for providing me with a digital copy and to Nick Sturm for the original discovery.

11   Maria Damon, 'John Wieners in the matrix of Massachusetts institutions: a psychopoeticgeography', *Journal of Beat Studies*, 3: 69–92, 2014.

12   Michael Seth Stewart, *'For the Voices': The Letters of John Wieners* (2014). *CUNY Academic*

with the Stonewall Uprising: Shively, four years younger than Wieners and a professor at Boston State College, was also an anarchist and an early pioneer of the Boston gay rights movement. Upon his release, Shively took Wieners to meetings and social events of the Boston Student Homophile League, introducing him to a new circle of younger queer activists which rejuvenated his work.[13]

Through such friendships, Wieners found himself part of a new, post-Stonewall surge of gay publishing and activism in Boston, whose radical critique of American society and its institutions had been suggested in the bohemian circles of 1960s American poetry, but was now given an internationalist and intersectional orientation within an explicitly queer context. Though there could be gendered tensions between gays and lesbians, and the whiteness of the Gay Liberation Movement received criticism, links were being drawn between older gay male traditions and emerging intersectional politics of Third-Worldism and feminism to expressions of queer, trans and 'genderfuck' identity.[14] In 1971, a group including Shively, Wieners, Michael Bronski and John Mitzel formed the Boston gay newsletter *Fag Rag*. With Shively at the centre, the collective was run on an anarchist, cooperative basis, with a core of members, as well as visiting or occasional participants. It was in Boston that the Combahee River Collective was formed in 1974 by a group of Black lesbian feminists who would play vital roles in the development of a new politics focused on the hitherto neglected role of queer women of colour, and the *Fag Rag* collective shared offices at 22 Bromfield Street with *Gay Community News*, members of whom were also involved with the Combahee Collective.[15] Mirroring the publishing processes of the Women's and Black Arts Movements, *Fag Rag* was part of a nationwide network of papers in Detroit, San Francisco and New York. Brightly coloured and militant in both its politics and aesthetics, the magazine featured essays, letters, activist reports, poems and visual art which often bordered on the pornographic. Seen as too trashy and working class for some – Susan Sontag apparently said that the magazine needed to reach a broader audience – *Fag Rag* was at one point described by New Hampshire governor Meldrim Thomson as 'the most loathsome publication in the English language'.[16] But Wieners – listed as a collective member in some issues, though his exact contribution is unclear – revelled in appearing in such

---

Works. Online <https://academicworks.cuny.edu/gc_etds/292> (456).

13   Stewart, 'For the Voices', 490–1.

14   See, e.g., Allen Young, 'Gay women and men: how we relate', *Gay Sunshine* 21: 8–9, spring 1974; Christopher Lonc, 'Genderfuck and its delights', *Gay Sunshine* 21: 4–16, spring 1974; Charley Shively, 'Fag Rag: the most loathsome publication in the English language', in *Insider Histories of the Vietnam Era Underground Press, Part 2*, ed. Ken Wachsberger (Ann Arbor, MI: Michigan University Press, 2012).

15   Charley Shively, 'Sequins and switchblades: in extremis exegesis. A reading of John Wieners' *Selected Poems, 1958–1984*, *Fag Rag* 44: 28–33 (29), 1984.

16   Shively, 'Fag Rag…', 2012.

company, his poems, essays and other unclassifiable texts frequently appearing under the name Jacqueline Wieners.

In 1972, members of the *Fag Rag* group, again with Shively at the centre, started the Good Gay Poets, the name a pun on Walt Whitman's famous designation as the 'Good Gray Poet'.[17] Their second publication was Wieners' joyous poem 'Playboy', recording the visit made by members of the *Fag Rag* collective to the 1972 Democratic Convention in Miami and delineating the new context Wieners had found. 'I delight in sharing group feeling. / Evening vigils, drag queens, movie actors, marijuana', he writes, linking this socialised vision of love to the personal and social love of the 1950s: 'New love, encountered between strangers / maybe or it's old love come back.'[18]

Typesetting, labour and queer collaboration

Such contexts gave Wieners' work a new political charge, as his poems began to articulate a class-conscious, psychiatric survivor identity suggesting the need for revolutionary change.[19] But the queer politics of this work also operate in terms of form, when it is at its most obtuse, as well as when it is direct. Around 1969, Wieners had begun experimenting with form, typography and voicing in ways not seen in his work since his earliest, generally unpublished poems.[20] Raymond Foye, who would go on to edit Wieners' next two books, noted in 1984:

> [H]e's after a reductive, abbreviated expression ... If a typo creeps in, he insists it stay. If I mistakenly break a line while typing up a new poem, that must stay, too. If I can't decipher a word & ask him what it is, he looks into the aether and pulls down a word that is as much of a non sequitur as possible. It's all an open-ended flux.[21]

Wieners worked closely with Charley Shively on *Behind the State Capitol*, a process Shively later documented in the essay 'JohnJob', published in the 1985 Wieners issue of the magazine *Mirage*.[22] As Shively notes, when Good

17 Shively, *'Fag Rag ...'*, lists the original group as including 'Aaron Shurin, Ron Schreiber, myself, David Eberly, Charles River, and John LaPorta', to which Michael Bronski adds Sal Farinella, Walta Borawski, Rudy Kikel and David Emerson Smith (author's interview with Michael Bronski, London, Dec. 2019).

18 *CAIB*, 124.

19 *SP*, 17–18.

20 For this early poetry, see the eight uncollected poems in *Floating Bear*, 10, 1961; 'A Proposition' (unpublished poem, May 1957), in *Letters, with Poems, to Michael Rumaker, 1955–1958*, *Battersea Review*, online <http://thebatterseareview.com/critical-prose/218-letters-with-poems-to-michael-rumaker-1955-58>; and 'End chapters in autobiography' and 'The bridge word', *Chicago Review*, 12 (1), spring 1958.

21 Quoted in Andrea Brady, '"Making use of this pain": the John Wieners Archive', *Paideuma* 36 (1–2): 131–79, 2007–9.

22 Charley Shively, 'JohnJob: editing *Behind the State Capitol or Cincinnati Pike*', *Mirage: John Wieners Issue*, 78–82, 1985.

Gay Poets published *State Capitol*, 'the work signalled an emerging energy and possibility of gay publishing, which had yet to be realised'. Despite the appearance of gay poetry anthologies such as Winston Leyland's 1975 *Angels of the Lyre*, large-scale collections of explicitly queer poetry like Wieners' were few and far between. As Shively writes, 'in 1974 & 75 we were only beginning to create our own medium'.[23] Wieners could have published with more established presses, and would later publish two full-length, career-spanning books with Black Sparrow. But, as Shively suggests, after the manuscript was turned down by Jonathan Cape, who'd published his previous *Selected Poems*, Wieners 'looked to the Good Gay Poets because it was not established, because it represented a coming to flower of newly released and previously unrehearsed energies.'[24]

Inspired by underground publications of the 1960s mimeo revolution like Ed Sanders' *Fuck You: A Magazine of the Arts*, a complete run of which Wieners gave to Shively as inspiration, Shively saw *Fag Rag* and the Good Gay Poets as a way to 'bring total freedom to authors, allowing each of us to write whatever and however we wished. What we needed most was not respect from the straight world but respect for each other's work.'[25] This goes completely against accounts that saw *State Capitol* as an embarrassing example of mental disintegration – which included not only those of Black Sparrow publisher John Martin, with its veiled homophobia, but of Wieners' friend and queer poetic colleague Robert Duncan.[26] Wieners *wanted* his work to appear this way.

State Capitol emerged in close collaboration with the publishers, its juxtaposition of lyric poetry, multiple voices, queer collages, class consciousness, gossip and high camp and – in particular – its visual appearance clearly reflecting the *Fag Rag* aesthetic. The 'cinema decoupages' of the book's subtitle refer both to the book's collages – collaborations between Wieners, Shively and John Mitzel – and to the poems in which words, letters and phrases are 'cut out', creating new juxtapositions and ambiguities. Wieners had worked on the manuscript for some years with an intern from Boston College: 'hacking, stuffing and reshelving' rather than making 'improvements'. This process of revising earlier, previously published texts reflected Wieners' general practice for years afterwards of annotating and decoupaging his own copies of his published books, from which he would improvise at public readings (Shively notes Wieners reading in this way at St Mark's Poetry Project as early as 1968). The cheapness of the book's design, resulting from the relative lack of resources for a grassroots publisher, happily merged with Wieners' own aesthetic practice and with the collective, collaborative nature of its publication.

---

23 Shively, 'JohnJob', 78.
24 Ibid.
25 Ibid.
26 Dunn, *Mesmerizing Apparition*, 43.

Wieners' longest book to date was produced in conditions of ephemerality that were embraced in creative ways. Using a rented IBM machine, the collective learned on the job. As Shively notes, 'Everyone struggled through learning the machine; those who knew how to use it passed what they had learned on to others.'[27] Alan Davies initially typeset the book on a compugraphic machine, but because the fluid was stale, the text literally vanished in the hot summer weather. Following this disaster, Rick Kinam reset the work flush left on the IBM typesetting machine, creating a series of chance line breaks in poems with longer lines which Wieners, liking their 'random and jumpy quality', insisted on retaining. Shively would take each variant spelling or spacing to Wieners throughout the process. Wieners found this irritating – as he put it, he would hold it against the publishers if there were *no* mistakes in the book.[28] He also revised conventional spellings to provide additional layers of meaning – thus, 'exhaustion' becomes 'exhausation' in order to emphasise breathlessness. The boundaries between 'intentional' and 'unintentional' variants – all held against a normative standard of grammar and spelling and typesetting – were deliberately broken down. Whether or not Wieners 'intended' such variants when he initially wrote the poems, retaining them reflected an adherence to error dating back at least as far as 1963, when he had written to publisher Robert Wilson: 'Tell the printer that everything in the book is as it should be. Mistakes in grammar, punctuation and spelling: (surrended, for surrendered) are intentional, or absolute as this is what the poem demanded. That is true to the experience of the poem.'[29] As Alan Davies comments, 'He holds that the inspiration of the writing is principal and should survive beyond formal consideration. Errors are a sign of human activity, perhaps inspiring trust or sympathy, instead of misunderstanding or derision.'[30] This defence of error is a lovely way of putting it. If the reader acts with a feeling for the poem's mood, an ear to its humour, its love and its terror, this becomes a collaborative process. The book's dizzying fantasy logic – in which movie stars become family members or friends or politicians, all of whom can also become the poet – was read by some as a solipsistic record of a mind closed off from the interactions of the real world. But it's more helpfully read as a kind of hypersocialised individuality: the visible emergence of the social into the individual, or the explosion of the two, in the (sexual, pathological, communitarian) refusal of boundaries. Valued as tenets of canonical modernism, such aspects are pathologised and dismissed in the work of a queer, gender non-conforming, working-class poet like Wieners.

The Good Gay Poets' collaborative, creative approach to typesetting relates to the often-feminised labour of typesetting in general, on which Sam Solomon writes illuminatingly in a recent essay on Bay Area lesbian

27   Shively, 'JohnJob', 80–1.
28   Ibid., 81.
29   Stewart, 'For the Voices', 324–5. 'The book' refers to *Ace of Pentacles*.
30   Alan Davies, 'An hardness prompts literature', 36.

feminist and socialist poet Karen Brodine, herself a typesetter. As Solomon notes, during the 1970s, changed employment practices, effected by shifts in typesetting technology, saw the increased hiring of 'de-skilled' and lower-paid feminised employees, with the by-product of 'tolerance' for non-normative sexual identities, an attitude Brodine sarcastically ventriloquises: 'it's so laid-back we don't have to dress up / & they don't even mind gays working here'.[31] At the same time, access to new modes of printing technology enabled the flourishing of LGBTQ+ small-press literary production during the 1970s and 1980s, operating on collective, low-cost principles, even as such ventures were constantly at risk from the very features that enabled them (racialised and gendered diversification of the labour force, changes in technology and precarious conditions).[32] Brodine's poem 'Line Corrections' has marked visual similarities with Wieners' work from *State Capitol*, even if its tone is rather different. Taken from an interview with 'Leola S' (typesetter Karen B), the poem consists of lines corrected from an interview transcript on labour history and workplace struggle, the resultant collage effect adding to its poetic urgency. Each stanza ends with a single word spaced across an entire line, an effect used to often disorientating purposes in Wieners' work. Thus, Brodine:

>   starting pay 1.53 per
>
>   h   o   u   r
>
>   [...]
>
>   she and some co-workers
>
>   today more than ever in US
>
>   h   i   s   t   o   r   y
>
>   ('Line Corrections')[33]

And Wieners:

>   [...] L ET IT BE S A I D
>
>   goldberg Mellons
>
>   make M o n e y, without reason, though attenuation begets
>   square dollar
>   c   R   U   S   T.
>
>   ('Aila's LASt WILL and T E S T A M E N T')[34]

31   Karen Brodine, 'Opposites that bleed one into the other or collide', *Heresies Magazine Issue #7: Women Working Together,* vol. 252–3, 1979, repr. in *Woman at the Machine, Thinking* (Seattle, WA: Red Letter Press, 1990).

32   Sam Solomon, 'Offsetting queer literary labor', *GLQ: A Journal of Lesbian and Gay Studies,* 24 (2): 239–66, 2018.

33   Brodine, 'Opposites that bleed', 16, 1990.

34   *BTSC,* 128. Compare the original printing of the poem in *Fire Exit* 3, eds. William Corbett and Fanny Howe, 29, 1973, in which statements are ordered within a clear, three-line stanza

In both cases, attention is drawn to the material fact of typesetting itself. Wieners deconstructs names so that readers pay attention to the social construction of (and performed by) language, linking the death of the immensely wealthy heiress Ailsa Mellon Bruce to capitalist exploitation more generally. The poem is preoccupied with the letter of the law – the language that enables the 'will' of the wealthy while denying that of the poor – while 'testament' recalls the class character of testifying under compulsion (from the Lavender Scare and McCarthyism to the police station and the asylum). For her part, Brodine emphasises both the character of labour described in the interview and the (gendered, racialised and classed) labour of typesetting that must be done to the transcript itself. This is a queered materialism, as both writers denaturalise the processes of labour, language, publication and revision that too often go unremarked.

Of course, such work rarely conforms to the standards of bosses, critics or heterosexuals. What Shively calls 'the intense scrutiny of the poetry police' is anticipated in *State Capitol* itself. Wieners ventriloquises:

> Get him out of my head, now they quote
> he's a GREat poet, put him back to hbed.
> Get rid of him.[35]

In July 1982, the run-down office building shared by *Fag Rag, Gay Community News* and the Good Gay Poets was firebombed by a group of laid-off firemen and policemen who had set a number of arson attacks in the city, 'protesting' cuts to the emergency services. On witnessing the fire, Shively, Bronski and others suspected a hate crime relating to a recent demonstration calling for the abolition of the city vice squad, in conjunction with real estate developers seeking to 'redevelop' the area. Given the frequent homophobic attacks on the offices – in Shively's words, 'mysterious break-ins, bullet holes, phone threats of death and fire so frequent, soon our back windows were totally gone, replaced by aluminium and then iron bows intended to keep out the storms' – such fears were entirely reasonable (and worked in favour of both police and real estate, whatever the culprits' immediate motivations).[36] All but a few hundred of the remaining copies of *State Capitol* were destroyed in the fire, an event Shively would later interpret in the pages of *Gay Sunshine* as the book's 'definitive exegesis': 'Here was revealed the void, the ashes, the destruction, the devastation. John Wieners had lived it first in his mind, in his poems, in his body.'[37] For Shively, the very real violence faced by the book's publishers is of a piece with the violence of erasure and dismissal afforded

---

structure, full or near-rhymes, and syntax contained within line breaks. The original reads simply: 'Let it be said Mellons make money, without reason, / though attenuation begets square dollar crust.'

35 'S E Q U E L T O AP O E M F OR PAINTERS', *BTSC*, 77. Spellings and capitalisation as per original.

36 Shively, 'Sequins and switchblades', 30.

37 Ibid., 33.

Behind the State Capitol and Wieners' later work in general. This chapter will now examine how such violence suffuses both the book itself and its critical reception through Wieners' gender identity and his experience of incarceration within mental health institutions.

'As the most beautiful woman in the world': naming, performance and gender as revision[38]

> To the conservatives and bigots, the state psychiatrists, the entrapment police, these gender switches must seem like ultimate perversions.
>
> (Robert Peters)[39]

Throughout *Behind the State Capitol*, Wieners celebrates and performs 'as' female celebrities, first ladies, heiresses and film stars such as Lana Turner, Greta Garbo, Billie Holiday, Marlene Dietrich, Barbara Hutton, Ailsa Mellon Bruce and, perhaps above all, Jacqueline Bouvier Kennedy Onassis ('REAd [...] to 400 listeners by The Voice of Greta Garbo, 1974 / P L A Z A').[40] Revision here reads as the re-vision (re-seeing) of gender identity, whether in the book's visual collages, or in the way the texts themselves juxtapose different voices through experimental typography, elaborate puns and verbal free association. The femme identifications of Wieners' work post-1969, in particular, are only now being acknowledged as 'proto-trans'.[41] Yet within those queer communities that offered the few extant contemporary responses to such work, such identities were already understood, explored and expressed. This was because publications like *Gay Sunshine* and *Fag Rag* took full advantage of the post-Stonewall liberation of sexual and gender identification, exploring in visuals and words 'genderfuck', drag and trans identities. Robert Peters' 1976 'The poet as drag "Quean"', an early review of *State Capitol*, explores the full range of Wieners' female voicings, from 'high camp' performances which display their own artifice (such as an 'imaginary interview' between Simone de Beauvoir and 'Great' Garbo) to 'genderfuck' manifestations such as the impersonation of Billie Holiday in 'Gardenias'.[42] As Peters writes, 'not only is [Wieners] homosexual [...] but unlike most gays (contrary to the clichés) he

---

38 Title of an uncollected poem published in *Fag Ray/Gay Sunshine: Stonewall 5th Anniversary Issue*, 25, summer 1974.
39 Robert Peters, 'The poet as drag "Quean"', *Mirage: John Wieners Issue*, 75–7 (77).
40 'To the bad debts', *BTSC*, 98.
41 See Trace Peterson and T.C. Tolbert, *Troubling the Line: Trans and Genderqueer Poetry and Poetics* (New York: Nightboat Books, 2013), 21. See also Nat Raha, 'Queer labour in Boston: the work of John Wieners, gay liberation and Fag Rag', in *Poetry and Work: Work in Modern and Contemporary Anglophone Poetry*, eds. Jo Lindsay Walton and Ed Lukers (London: Palgrave Macmillan, 2019), 195–243. Wieners can be read as a trans identity, retaining masculine pronouns.
42 *BTSC*, 168–70 (62).

feels more female than he does male.'[43] Likewise, Shively's 'What happened to the mind of John Wieners?', published in *Gay Sunshine* in 1977, responds to the pathologisation of Wieners and his work partially through noting its gender non-conformity. De-essentialising gender, Shively notes Wieners' rejection of the 'callus [sic] male principle', preventing feelings of love and affection, and encountered in Wieners' unrequited crushes or affairs with closeted, married 'heterosexual' men, and focus on qualities associated with the feminine, including Marian devotion and the figure of the mother. For Shively: 'The woman-identified poet is rare even among women and perhaps unique among men. This identification gives a special cast to the gayness of John Wieners.'[44]

Yet subsequent assessments of this work have failed to grasp Wieners' gender identity. Correctly eliding its experimental technique with its gender non-conformity, critics do so in a borderline homo-/transphobic manner, their scrutiny paralleling that of the mental health professionals who policed Wieners' speech, bearing and behaviour, plying him with electroshock and heavy doses of drugs with damaging and debilitating side effects. The characterisations pile up: Wieners manifests 'male hysteria'; his female 'drag [is] tacked onto an evidently male canvas'; his 'transvestite sensibility' avoids 'the social cost of actually being a woman'; 'Wieners articulates an infantile position'; he presents 'another screen, a defenceless persona whose theatricality itself served as a form of defence'. Here is an excerpt from one such reading of Wieners' prose poem 'Woman' (1970): 'Wieners speaks, finally, like any queer postmodern, from a transvestite sensibility about WOMAN, without the social cost of actually being a woman who functions inside systems of male privilege and masculine ideologies.'

For this critic, Wieners' text exemplifies 'masculinities' that can 'be ephebic, get feminine, dress in drag at will', without facing the 'social cost(s)' of an assumed, essential femininity. Leaving aside the assumptions about 'actually being' a particular binary gender, some background on the 'treatments' prescribed to gay people in the mental institutions of the time will quickly disabuse us of this notion of 'social cost'. 'Aversion therapy' involved the administration of electrical shock to the genitalia of patients when they became aroused upon being shown queer pornography: combined with the homophobic prejudices of talk therapists, the practice is memorably satirised in poet Judy Grahn's 1964 'The Psychoanalysis of Edward the Dyke.'[45] Wieners was repeatedly 'treated' with electroshock, lithium, insulin injections and other forced medication that severely damaged his memory and sense of creativity, and threatened with 'electrical catheter treatment', as painfully attested by letters written to Charles Olson and other friends in 1961, desperately pleading that they help him get released from Medfield State

43   Peters, 'The poet as drag "Quean"', 76.
44   Shively, 'What happened to the mind of John Wieners', 1977.
45   On such techniques, see Don Jackson, 'Dachau for queers', *Gay Sunshine* 1(3), Nov. 1970.

Hospital, to which his parents had forcibly committed him – a 40-day stay had turned into a six-month incarceration.[46] Visiting Wieners during another institutionalisation (this time in Central Islip Hospital, Long Island) at the end of the decade, visitors Anne Waldman and Bill Berkson were horrified to see the heavy administration of drugs and the regimented and crowded sleeping conditions. As Waldman noted, it was astonishing that anyone could write poetry at all in such surroundings.[47] As Charley Shively would later write, 'The authorities [...] have blasted his brain with chemicals, electricity, and outright demands that HE NOT WRITE. Having done nothing to ease his life, they have failed to silence his voice.'[48]

When exploring this work, the reader discovers the horrific violence faced by feminised subjects within a patriarchal, homo- and transphobic institutional apparatus. The critics who condemn Wieners' apparent male privilege appear to overlook such treatment in favour of going after their victim. It's worth noting, too, that this line of criticism is very much part of the growing transphobia of the time, culminating in Janice Raymond's notorious *The Transsexual Empire*, a book which emerged from her dissertation, supervised by Mary Daly at Boston College, and published in 1979 by Boston-based radical publisher Beacon Press. For Wieners, by contrast, in lines at once defiant and despairing:

> I don't know anything about being a man, or a woman.
> Only about being a poet, in love with one man,
> no youth, future, or past. I speak to you off the network[49]

In the face of intensive surveillance, punishment and gender policing, Wieners' insistent feminine identifications are acts not of 'appropriation', but of courage.

Placing this work in the context of the gender politics expressed in publications such as *Fag Rag* and *Gay Sunshine* further undermines the borderline-transphobic readings to which it has been subjected. In a 1974 essay called 'Genderfuck and its delights', published in *Gay Sunshine*, Christopher Lonc carefully distinguishes between drag performers, tolerated or mocked within the 'straight world', and 'genderfuck' as a rejection of gendered social roles in general, expressed in particular (but not only) through clothing. Lonc details the abuse faced, not only from the usual homophobic sources, but also from those in the Gay Liberation Movement:

> One of the most common things people shout at me on the street is: 'Are you a boy or a girl?' I hope that people listen to themselves. That is exactly what my life is all about. It is my

46   Stewart, 'For the Voices', 268–9.
47   Waldman, quoted in Dunn, 'Mesmerizing Apparition', 22; Berkson, *Since When: A Memoir in Pieces* (Minneapolis, MN: Coffee House Press, 2018).
48   Shively, 'What happened to the mind of John Wieners', 3.
49   'White Slavery', *BTSC*, 84.

choice to not be a man, and it is my choice to be beautiful. I am not a female impersonator; I don't want to mock women. I want to criticize and poke fun at the roles of women and of men too. I want to try and show how not-normal I can be. I want to ridicule and destroy the whole cosmology of restrictive sex roles and sexual identification.[50]

Extending beyond ideas of drag as humorous parody – dismissed by heterosexuals and accused of sexism by sections of the gay and feminist movements – Lonc's concept of 'genderfuck' identifies those who cross gender lines as the most militant faction within the queer movement because they are the first to 'get their heads bashed in' and the least able to remain 'closeted'. Lonc's work is an important part of the history of non-binary identity as it existed before currently available terminology. Emphasising the presence of non-binary, working-class queers in the key moments of Gay Liberation, such as Stonewall, it rewrites conventional feminist and queer accounts which refuse to take into account non-binary gender identities.

Wieners' gender non-conformity is also clearly present from his earliest work: examples include poems concerning drag queens – 'Ballade' (1955), or 'Times Square' (1969) – and those concerning his own gender identification such as 'The Woman in Me' (1959), 'Memories of You' (1965) and 'Feminine Soliloquy' (1969).[51] Yet these elements are virtually absent from critical reception. Anecdotes of Wieners' penchant for feminised dress and femme outrageousness rarely politicise such actions, tending from the sympathetic (Amiri Baraka, Bill Berkson) to the pathologising, such as Hilary Holladay's portrait of bohemian degeneration ('His eyes heavy with mascara, he would stroll up and down the streets in a drugged torpor').[52] In fact, there were immense risks to such gender non-conformity. Basil King recalls an occasion when he and Wieners – the latter 'all gadded out in high heels' – had to flee a bar near Black Mountain College. In King's words: 'Both of us realized that if we were running and they caught us they'd kill us.'[53] Whether outright murdered by homophobes, or having committed suicide in despair, lives like Wieners' were intensely vulnerable, as recorded in the heartbreaking 'Ballade', first published in the *Boston Newsletter*, in which the drag queen Alice O'Brien ends up hanged in her jail cell.

In order to understand his own gender identity, Wieners at times appears to deploy the vocabulary of 'inversion' that earlier queer writing had

50 Lonc, 'Genderfuck and its delights'.

51 *Boston Newsletter*, n.p.; *SP,* 117; *The Journal of John Wieners is to be called 707 Scott Street, for Billie Holiday* (Los Angeles, CA: Sun and Moon Press, 1996 [1959]), 20–1; *CAIB*, 58–9; *SP*, 159.

52 Hilary Holladay, *Herbert Huncke: The Times Square Hustler Who Inspired Jack Kerouac and the Beat Generation* (Tucson, AZ: Schaffner Press, 2015). See also Bill Berkson, *Since When*, and *Amiri Baraka and Ed Dorn: The Complete Letters*, ed. Claudia Moreno Pisano (Albuquerque, NM: University of New Mexico Press, 2014), 120. For an exception to this critical norm, see Raha, 'Queer labour in Boston'.

53 Quoted in Stewart, 'For the Voices' 10.

inherited from Krafft-Ebing, Edward Carpenter and Havelock Ellis ('I have a woman's mind / in a man's body'; 'there's a certain kind of men / born to suffer as women'[54]). Yet Wieners' texts of the 1970s in particular exceed such categories; they are much closer to 'genderfuck', or to what Trace Peterson calls 'proto-trans'. Aspiring to be, and often ventriloquising, a wealthy female film star or heiress, Wieners critiques naturalised modes of gender performance and autobiographical explanation, quipping to Raymond Foye that he is 'borrowing heavily for my own autobiography' from the memoirs of stripper Blaze Starr.[55] Frequently, the connective 'as', in the manner of film credits, links one person's performance 'as' another character. 'Where was I as Greta Garbo?', asks one poem, and Wieners 'signs' an early version of 'Ailsa's Last Will and Testament' with 'Gusta L. (Garbo) Gustafson', fusing in this signature the original and stage names of a notoriously reclusive Hollywood star. Doing this additionally destabilises the idea of authentic legal record, since Garbo appends her own name to heiress Ailsa Mellon Bruce's will.[56] Wieners' film-star fascination emerges from the pages of movie magazines and gossip columns, texts which are all about the interplay of private and public: transgressing the boundaries, revealing what lies behind the curtain, offering readers a privileged, aspirational glimpse into the lives of the rich and (in)famous which might also mean voyeuristic access to abjection. Wieners often focuses on female celebrities whose glamour has faded, fodder for occasional gossip column exposés in women's and movie magazines with titles like 'What happened to the mind of Jennifer Jones?' These texts bring out the visceral disgust of such fascination, in which the collapse of an 'ideal' body must be hidden from sight, yet, precisely thanks to its hiddenness, becomes the subject of a kind of fascinated horror. 'Alida Valli' begins as a parodically complimentary movie magazine profile of the Italian actor ('the woman who I worshipped for thirty years'), before shifting to Valli's physical 'decline'.

> [...] What is wrong with Valli, anyway?
> 10 days, and I have been intermittently pondering, ear-
> lier my cause for her mind and anatomy to chalk up, as
> below par. The reason?
>   Hepatitus [sic], too many writhings owing from child-bearing,
> world-position pertinently, worst assumption verified. The
> Hispanic child-rack. A particular punishment, inflicted upon
> higher primates resulting in deterioration.[57]

The tone here can come across as waspish and cruel – or as a satire on the

---

54 'Memories of You', *CAIB*, 59; 'Yours to Take', *BTSC*, 133.
55 *CAIB*, 15. This fascination went back to Wieners' earliest writing: see the early, unpublished poem 'A Proposition' (1957) (Stewart, *Letters, with Poems to Michael Rumaker*).
56 Wieners, 'Trying to Forget', *BTSC*, 72, and 'Ailsa's Last Will and Testament' [1973], *Fire Exit*, 3: 29. A revised version of the latter poem appears in *BTSC*, 128e.
57 'Alida Valli', *BTSC*, 16.

waspish and cruel. While Wieners doesn't explicitly identify *as* Valli here, it makes sense to place the text's judgment on ageing in the context of his own life. Charley Shively would later note the importance of recognising this work as that of an 'ageing quean' – Wieners, who'd burst onto the scene while barely in his twenties, was now approaching middle age (he was nearly 42 when the book came out), physically marked by years of drug use, electroshock and poverty leading to the loss of most of his teeth: 'Most gay poetry tends to concentrate on the young: first love, break-ups, the sheer hedonistic delight in the feelings of romance, the dangers, fears and triumphs of gayness. Little has been seen said about the ageing quean. *What Happens Twenty Years Later* might be another subtitle to this book – a sustained meditation on ageing in the gay ghetto.'[58]

Collaging the memories of his past – a high school graduation photo, a poem written in 1952, old letters, reminiscences of youth in Boston or New York – with the present, and identifying with the ageing Valli, Lana Turner and Garbo, Wieners understands the beauty standards pressed upon feminised people, whether through the heteronormative expectations of child-bearing faced by Valli, or of youthful beauty within gay groupings. Further, Wieners understands that the construction of glamorous Hollywood identity, through clothes, make-up, plastic surgery and media coverage, may serve to alter the body painfully in a manner of which the 'rack' of childbirth is, in a sense, merely the inverse. Like many queer people, Wieners' Hollywood spectatorship is hardly simple: identifying with its images of idealised femininity, while aware of their cruel costs, and seeking to subvert the social codes they enforced through appropriative, camp and experimental strategies of his own. The lives of 'the rich and the super-rich' offer a sometimes painful contrast to Wieners' own sufferings as a 'child of the working class', and the two modes – desperate poverty and the apparent luxury of the rich – are used to undercut each other in the interests, ultimately, of a communal, queer aesthetic. This will render the movies' fantasies of pleasure more than their simply being pipe dreams underwritten by suffering, violence and decline.

'The problem of madness': Wieners as psychiatric survivor

As we've seen, much of the critical reception of Wieners' 1970s work rests on pathologising assumptions concerning gender identity. To conclude, I wish to examine Wieners' reaction to his incarceration within mental 'health' institutions, which he understood to be closely related to questions of gender and sexuality. In a 1973 interview with Shively, Wieners argues that the asylum violently enforces gender conformity, with patients punished if their behaviour does not conform to gender norms (arguably the reason many patients are in there in the first place):

58 Shively, 'What happened to the mind of John Wieners', 1977.

I would say that the homosexual is repugnant, repelled by others, even in the insane asylums. They're looked on as somewhat apart, more extravagant in gestures and mannerisms. Most of the women are oversized, usually with masculine characteristics. And the men seem to be underdeveloped as to an ideal manhood. I suppose they are in those institutions just because we have created stereotyped roles of what people should look like; what they should wear; how they should converse. Because these individuals fill none of these roles, they're incarcerated.[59]

Wieners protests such conditions both in explicitly political ruminations and in more disjunctive lyrics. In 1974, two short poems called 'Survivor' and '8 Verses' appeared in the *Poetry Project Newsletter*, and were subsequently reprinted in *State Capitol* as a single piece entitled 'E Doneilson'.[60] The original title to the first poem (see below) seems to pick up on the emergent discourse, spearheaded by Judi Chamberlin and the Mental Patients Liberation Front (MPLF), of patients and ex-patients as 'psychiatric survivors' (Wieners likely attended meetings of the Boston MPLF branch).[61]

Survivor

Coded; spaced out;
transvestited; in doubt
invert; Emily's skirt

no felled behavior
Travelled the border.
as exhibitions' route,
           p.22

This seems to be a description of the state of the patient – 'coded' and 'spaced out'. The psychiatrist tries to read the 'code' of the patient's words, often to reveal what they think they already know – that the patient is mentally ill, delinquent, sexually deviant. Wieners hallucinated 'coded', punning associations during his breakdowns, but these also characterise poetry's sound-based logics (here, for instance, the internal rhyme that leads from 'invert' to 'skirt'). 'Transvestited', a typically deft and complex pun, hangs somewhere between 'travestied', 'transvestite', 'transvested' (a rare back-

59 *SP*, 293.
60 Wieners, 'Survivor' and 'Eight Verses', *Poetry Project Newsletter* 13, 1 March 1974; repr. as 'E. Doneilson', *BTSC*, 58. My best guess to the title is that it refers to Barbara Deering Danielson, widow of *Atlantic Monthly* editor Richard Danielson, and Boston patron of the arts, but also a long-time member of the corporation of Massachusetts General Hospital, in whose psychiatric wing Wieners was institutionalised. (See Danielson's obituary, UPI, 1982, online <https://www.upi.com/Archives/1982/11/28/International-Harvester-heiress-Barbara-Deering-Danielson-has-died-following/2804407307600/>).
61 See Raha, 'Queer labour in Boston', 146, 236–7; *SP*, 293.

formation of transvestite), and 'invested' – both cross-dressing and being clothed with authority – leading to 'invert', with its echoes of the Krafft-Ebing model of homosexuality. Potentially, these first three lines read as though addressed to the psychiatrist-critic: [if you are] 'in doubt' as to my gender identity, 'invert' or reverse it. 'Emily's skirt' might suggest Emily Dickinson – the 'transvestited', feminised poet wearing Dickinson's skirt, taking on her identity, assuming her authority but also her marginalisation, doubting and being held in doubt. (Note, too, that Dickinson was a key part of the pantheon of 'women poets' – Edna St Vincent Millay, Sara Teasdale, Elinor Wylie and H.D. – to whom Wieners 'responded first' as a young poet, attracted to 'their observations of nature, to their love feeling, and to an abbreviation of expression.'[62])

Following the stanza break, the apparent non-sequitur 'no felled behavior' perhaps refers back to the titular idea of survival – the survivor will not be felled, will stand tall. Meanwhile, 'travelled the border' suggests going close to an edge – of madness, of what's acceptable gendered behaviour. Combining with apparent found text – 'as exhibitions' route, // p.22' – there is a sense of being on display, exhibited, forced to follow a particular path, as well as of a voice from elsewhere. Through its dense, elliptical puns and 'abbreviat[ed] expression', the poem has much to say about being on display, performance, clothing and perception, as these relate to gender and mental health. Its grammatical compression – deliberately missing words, so that the link between subject, object and action is almost always unclear – becomes a way of resisting the normative gaze, while also speaking in code, of one's gender or neuro non-conformity.

Whether or not this poem was written from psychiatric incarceration, that experience hangs over it, because and not in spite of its obliquity. During Wieners' frequent incarcerations, the very act of writing a poem became something to be wrested from the hands of, or from under the noses of, the authorities, and one might (without overstretching the point) read such obscurity as in part a reaction to such censorship. But Wieners was also writing more obviously political poems denouncing the mental health system. The most famous of these is undoubtedly 'Children of the Working Class'.[63] The poem was written on May Day 1972, 'from incarceration, Taunton State Hospital'. Wieners sent the poem to Douglas Calhoun, editor of *Athanor* magazine, but was forced to change the original version after reading the poem out loud in group therapy. He amended 'Taunton State Hospital' to the word 'Staid' – an ironic verbal echo on 'state', meaning 'sedate, respectable, unadventurous', as well as being the past tense of the verb 'to stay', thus also meaning the condition of confinement – which defies enforced linguistic silencing through an ironised self-description of the process. Wieners wrote the poem on the institution's typewriter, so could not prepare the poem to

62　*SP*, 296.
63　*BTSC*, 34–5.

send to Calhoun without making this change – in the end, he managed to keep the original (and crucial) location marker by means of a phone call. Calhoun paints a vivid picture of these conditions, in which authorial control and enforced revision were closely related to institutional suppression: 'Wieners called three or four times, odd hours. Picture him in some corner of the hospital, a deserted office, making calls, glancing over his shoulder, about poetry'.[64]

In the piece quoted near the beginning of this chapter, George Butterick, from whom the story about the poem's composition is drawn, criticises the typographical choices made when the poem was reprinted in *Behind the State Capitol*. Butterick, who compiled a bibliography of Wieners' extant work which was published alongside the poem in *Athanor* in 1972, feels that Wieners' recent editors have done a disservice to his work, spoiling its previous 'rough genius' and 'naivete'.[65] He zooms in on the start of the second stanza – 'there are worse, whom you may never see, non crucial around / the / spoke'. For Butterick, removing 'the' to a line on its own is entirely random, and depletes the rhythmic force of the poem's long lines. The 'spoke' puns on Boston's nickname as 'the hub' – but 'spoke' obviously relates to speech as well. As John Wilkinson notes, the stuttering pause created by placing the definite article on its own emphasises the poet's doubleness. Wieners is both the speaker of the poem – the one who 'spoke', in an act of confession – and as a psychiatric patient, is 'the always spoken for'.[66] Moving 'the' onto its own line may simply have been the result of what Shively notes – the shunting over of words on to the next line, sometimes even their splitting, as a result of the flush left typesetting (this is seen later in the poem with the line-breaks on words with 'o' – 'blo/ated, t/o, g/od, n/o'). Yet it also assumes a function as a combination – and does it matter? – of accident and design, on the precipice of the spoken and the textual, in the midst of the institution. Such speech, in the context of the asylum, also links to the poem's second line: 'gaunt, ugly deformed / broken from the womb, and horribly shriven / at the labour of their forefathers' (a reference to Catholic confession) – the Church and the State apparatus of the asylum unite to persecute the working-class mental patient. To 'shrive' is to present oneself to a priest for confession, penance or absolution; so to be shriven is to have confessed. The asylum is infantilising: like the Church, it requires confession, in an atmosphere of shame, secrecy and surveillance.

There's a pun here too on labour as birth and labour as class identity – remember that the poem was written on May Day – and the poem as a whole constructs a despairing lineage of the exploited, the downtrodden and the mental costs they suffer. The opening dedication, 'to Somes', puns

64   Calhoun, quoted in George Butterick, 'Editing postmodern texts', *Sulfur* 11: 129–30, 1981.
65   Butterick, 'Editing postmodern texts'.
66   John Wilkinson, 'A superficial examination of the work of John Wieners', *Mirage: John Wieners Issue*, 110–15 (112).

on mathematical sums, anticipating the later line-break on those who are 'crudely numb/ered before the dark of dawn'. Wieners elsewhere writes about the debt his parents incurred from his hospitalisation, and there too 'sums' highlights the economic conditions in which patients are treated as statistics, or as broken parts of sums who must be 'added up' into normative subjects. And, as 'Somes', they are also explicitly 'some' and not 'others' – their situation is particular to their class. Wieners describes the patients 'locked in Taunton State Hospital and other peon work farms'. Institutional peonage was a widespread practice of employing patients to perform productive labour associated with the maintenance of the asylum, such as housekeeping or laundry duties, without adequate compensation. It was initially seen as vocational, a tool for assimilation back into society when patients were released, or as therapeutic, but as the State's underfunded asylums expanded, with more patients and fewer staff, it increasingly became an exploitative way of treating patients. As with the original meaning of peonage – a form of indentured or peasant labour practised in South America and the Deep South – asylum patients were essentially forced to perform free labour to pay off their debts. In this practice, the Victorian vocabulary of labour as productivity and moral worth justifies the exploitation of those who are supposedly being protected, encapsulated in the term deployed: 'moral therapy'.[67] As with prison labour, the 13th amendment to the Constitution could be circumvented in carceral circumstances. Growing outrage over this practice – and the activism of mental patients' groups, or, as they began to describe themselves, 'psychiatric survivors' – led to its abolition in some states during this period, but many cases remained mired in legislation for decades afterwards. In his May Day poem, Wieners, who knew this condition of indebtedness well, acutely links the ways in which class and labour play into the exploitation of mental health patients.[68] Wieners is not just arguing that conditions of poverty and shame make the children of the working class more likely to suffer from mental illness, but that those same children are also exploited for their labour *within* the asylum, exacerbating conditions of familial debt in a vicious circle, based on the institutions of work and mental health. Within *State Capitol*, the poem is placed immediately after 'For What Time Slays' – a poem written the day before Wieners' release from incarceration in 1961 – and before 'By the Bars', which links familial prohibition, class and mental illness. This placement contributes to a class-conscious, highly politicised argument that belies the apparent 'chaos' of the book's organisation, even if that logic is only partially revealed.

As a child of the working class, Wieners has been cheated from the rewards of his rightful labour; he has been cheated by his traumatic home life; and he is forever excluded from Whitman's vision of a democratic America and from

67 On institutional peonage, see F. Lewis Bartlett, 'Institutional peonage: our exploitation of mental patients', *Atlantic Monthly*, June 1964.
68 On debt, see *SP*, 226 and *BTSC*, 98.

a vision of Christian divine love. The poem ends:

> [...] I am witness
> not to Whitman's vision, but instead the
> poorhouses, the mad city asylums and re-
> lief worklines. Yes, I am witness not to
> God's goodness, but his better or less scorn.

This is a critique without resolution. The individual is a victim of both God and State, subject to divine scorn and left out of the vision of a democratic, inclusive America. Yet Wieners nonetheless refuses the asylum's vicious interpellations. The poem is an act not of 'confession', but of witnessing, of defiance. Rather than being observed, he observes, taking the power of language back into his hands, even as the asylum authorities try to stop him writing.

Wieners' involvement in 'mental patient liberation meetings' saw him take part in a movement in which patients and ex-patients perceived themselves as 'psychiatric survivors', as active subjects, rather than passive objects of 'treatment' and punishment, working to organise within and challenge the authoritarian aspects of mental health institutions.[69] Particularly influential here was the work of Judi Chamberlin, leader of the MPLF, whose book *On Our Own* posits alternative methods of care.[70] Influenced by Chamberlin, Erving Goffman, Michel Foucault, Thomas Szasz and, in particular, the controversial 'anti-psychiatrist' R.D. Laing, the process of de-institutionalisation of the 1970s was one way of challenging the oppressive nature of mental health institutions: for instance, institutional peonage was legally abolished the year after Wieners' poem was written, requiring that any work done by patients must be properly remunerated. Yet much of the exploitation that took place in the asylum continued elsewhere. Away from the repressive, disciplinary apparatus of both State and private institutions, patients were still vulnerable. This indicates some of the problems of challenging and dismantling institutions in general: what to replace them with, how to change society when the overall balance of power – whatever the particular institutions it manifests in – remains the same.

Likewise, the cooperative printing and organising enterprises of the Good Gay Poets, with their militant, often utopian energies, gave way to the desperate urgencies of Aids-era organising in the 1980s. As Michael Bronski remembers, 'reading through these journals and anthologies, it's impossible to not think about how many of these poets are now dead.'[71] For his part, Wieners lapsed into near silence, continually writing and supported by a network of close friends such as Shively, Jack Powers and Jim Dunn, but only rarely publishing or reading from his work. The poems of *Behind the State*

69　*SP*, 293.
70　Judi Chamberlin, *On Our Own: Patient Controlled Alternatives to the Mental Health System* (New York: Haworth Press, 1978).
71　Author's interview with Michael Bronski, London, Dec. 2019.

Capitol, like much of Wieners' other poetry about the asylum experience and about the poverty which 'has nearly ripped my life off', sometimes attest to despair, and the book's experimental processes of revision, typesetting and publication can make for difficult reading.[72] Yet this book is also reparative, utopian as much as despairing. These poems are acts of salvation, using humour, camp, non-sequiturs, 'genderfuck' identifications, movie-star performances, political screeds and heartbroken laments to challenge the exclusion and suppression of Wieners' class and gender identity within a rapidly gentrifying city. Such poetry is a space of solace, then and now: a true gift, for activists, queer scholars, poets and readers, if they'll have it, and one with much still to teach its readers about the ways in which class, gender and sexuality serve as both tools of oppression and beacons of hope.

72 'New Beaches', *CAIB*, 158.

2. Derek Jarman's queer histories: *Derek Jarman's Caravaggio*

Alexandra Parsons

Queer icon Derek Jarman (1942–94) was an interdisciplinary luminary best known for his films. He was also highly influential across his wider practice, which ranged from painting, set design and gardening to political activistm and writing, all of which are currently attracting renewed interest and analysis.

This chapter focuses on his writing, and on one lesser-known text in particular, *Derek Jarman's Caravaggio*, published alongside the release of the film *Caravaggio* in February 1986. Jarman wrote and published voraciously, creating a diverse body of unusual, hybrid books, many of them echoing the scrapbook form he used in his working sketchbooks.[1] He wrote the majority of these following his diagnosis as HIV-positive in December 1986, from which point on he urgently deployed his extraordinary creative energies to speak out against the resurgence of state-sanctioned homophobia in the 1980s after the HIV/Aids crisis began, and the reintroduction in Britain of legislative initiative 'Clause 28' in December 1987 (passed into law as Section 28 in May 1988). Jarman's own diagnosis has been widely viewed as the catalyst for his politicisation and the moment from which he became politically active. Yet his fascination with queer figures from the past, which far predates his diagnosis, demonstrates an existing political commitment to queer history as a means of making a claim for the strength and perseverance of queer identities. He repeatedly foregrounds queer identities from Western cultural history alongside his own personal history in his artistic practice, a preoccupation that would only become yet more critical during a period of enormous uncertainty, grief and suffering as the 1980s and '90s drew on.

Jarman's approach to the past was always provisional and always collage-based: he quickly gathered together different materials and subject matters and, by doing so, created polyvalent, multilayered works aimed at understanding and expanding the relationship between the past and present, and in particular articulating new ways of understanding how, in Jim Ellis's

---

1   See *Derek Jarman's Sketchbooks*, eds. Stephen Farthing and Edward Webb-Ingall (London: Thames & Hudson, 2013).

words, 'history inhabits and informs the present'.[2] Jarman, in his earliest feature films *Jubilee* and *The Tempest*, uses the moment of the English Renaissance in order to interrogate and satirise contemporary ideas of Englishness and the nation. Yet to understand his later sharply focused political engagement with our queer past, it is of benefit to return instead to his work on the life of the Baroque artist Michelangelo Merisi da Caravaggio, a project that had its genesis at the end of the 1970s. Jarman had immense difficulties obtaining the financing necessary for this, his next planned feature film, and he struggled over a period of years to attain the funding required while writing and rewriting scripts with a number of collaborators. He eventually made *Caravaggio* in 1985, and it was released early the following year. Characterised by its spare set (a warehouse in Limehouse), the film uses the framing device of the dying Michele Caravaggio being tended to by his mute assistant, as scenes from his life are recounted via a series of flashbacks. A number of these are formed from *tableaux vivants*: restagings both of Caravaggio's paintings and of other artists' work, including, for example, Jacques-Louis David's *Marat Assassiné* (1793).

The lavishly illustrated book *Derek Jarman's Caravaggio* emerged alongside the release of the film. It was the first of the books he published to accompany the release of a film – a practice he was to continue for the rest of his life. Like the later books, *War Requiem* (1989) and *Wittgenstein: The Terry Eagleton Script, the Derek Jarman Film* (1993), it contains a version of the film script, yet unlike those titles, it includes different kinds of text. The script itself is interspersed with Jarman's reflections on the violence and intensity of Caravaggio's life and art, information about the making of the film, and a series of autobiographical fragments about Jarman's life and work.[3] The text of *Derek Jarman's Caravaggio* acts as a complement to *Caravaggio* by expanding on its contents, laying out Jarman's approach to the biography of the painter, whereby Jarman recreated Caravaggio's paintings as a means of creating a narrative of his life. In *Derek Jarman's Caravaggio*, Jarman takes a queer figure from history as his starting point and intermingles the records of the past with the contemporary. At times, the technique works overtly to tie Jarman's own life to that of the Renaissance painter. In other instances, Jarman uses more oblique methods to comment on Caravaggio's paintings and, in particular, Caravaggio's self-representations.

The book is an artefact, distinct from the film that prompted its production, and echoes the beautiful large sketchbooks that Jarman kept throughout his working life. It operates as an activist text that excavates queer histories and acts as a means of protest in an unexpected form. At first glance *Derek Jarman's Caravaggio* seems an unlikely protest document. The book is slightly short

2   Jim Ellis, *Derek Jarman's Angelic Conversations* (Minneapolis, MN: University of Minnesota Press, 2009), viii.

3   This is a technique Jarman returns to in his later book, *Queer Edward II* (London: British Film Institute, 1991), published alongside the release of *Edward II*.

of A4 in size, and comprises 136 pages. It is full of photographs by Tunisian-American artist Gerald Incandela, mostly in black and white, with some full-colour plates of film stills. Yet like Jarman's films, it contains an array of rich imagery that has been hastily put together. It is a less expensive production than an art monograph, and the scrapbook-like form enables its experiments in representation and self-representation to shine.

This chapter analyses several elements of the Caravaggio project, beginning with Jarman's deeply personal use of the past as a way of finding and linking queer forebears to his own experience. He uses the text to advance what would become a refrain throughout the rest of his career: by intermingling alternative queer histories with the contemporary, he produces political contestation. Jarman placed his historical project in productive relation to Caravaggio's own iconoclastic historical project, in which the painter overlaid biblical and classical scenes with private meaning from his own life. Critically, *Derek Jarman's Caravaggio* highlights self-representational acts that are fleeting in the film – Caravaggio's self-portraits, as well as Jarman's self-conscious reflection on his role as painter and director during a brief cameo – allowing readers time to engage with them. He playfully interacts with Caravaggio's dismembered self-portraits in *Derek Jarman's Caravaggio*, speculating about the autobiographical meanings found within these grisly images. Jarman revisits the self-portraits as a means to claim them – and the choreographed staging of Caravaggio's personal life that they depict – for his own constructed queer history and, by extension, that of others in 1980s Britain. Most importantly, Jarman uses collage as a technique throughout the book to emphasise the way the film, like any other version of the painter's life, is just one possible construction or reading.

In the book, Jarman uses the opportunity that the film release presented to expand upon the connections between his life as a queer man in the present and that of Caravaggio, whose biographies often excised the queer elements of his life. He revises some of the autobiographical meanings presented by Caravaggio in order to make the historical figure's dramatic work speak to issues of queer representation in the early 1980s, including using the trope of queer martyrdom to highlight contemporary suffering and persecution. By insisting upon the connections between his life in the then present and Caravaggio's, one of a lineage of famous queer men, and by producing narratives that entangle his own past with those of that lineage, he attempted to counter some of the harm he suffered growing up in a Britain where sex acts between men were illegal, prejudice was rife, and information hard to come by.

Jarman was always invested in what Carolyn Dinshaw has summarised as 'a queer desire for history': he was driven to insist upon a queer past (using the terms of the present) and thereby forge community across time.[4] Yet he also, in doing this, displays a desire to enable different kinds of connections across

---

4   Carolyn Dinshaw et al., 'Theorizing queer temporalities roundtable', *GLQ: Journal of Lesbian and Gay Studies*, 13.2–3 (2007): 177–95 (178).

time and different – or queer – conceptions of time that permit ways of being historical which exceed linear time. For Elizabeth Freeman, engaging with queer temporalities involves 'mining the present for signs of undetonated energy from past revolutions', and it is this drive, as seen in *Derek Jarman's Caravaggio*, that this chapter unpacks.[5]

Jarman's use of the past: Caravaggio

Although it was not Jarman who originally chose Caravaggio as a subject but his producer, Nicholas Ward-Jackson, the artist was an appropriate choice for him. In his 1992 memoir *At Your Own Risk*, Jarman describes the deeply personal path always taken by his queer history project. Speaking of his self-education in the early 1960s while at King's College London, he comments: 'I began to read between the lines of history. The hunt was on for forebears who validated my existence.'[6] Caravaggio was just one of a list of queer forebears from this period in Europe who, throughout his career, Jarman explored and drew on. He asks, 'Was Western civilization Queer? The Renaissance certainly was. Lorenzo di Medici, Michelangelo, Leonardo, Botticelli, Rosso, Pontormo, Caravaggio, Shakespeare, Marlowe, Bacon.'[7] Jarman claims these prominent artists, writers and polymaths for a queer tradition. 'The point', as Pascale Aebischer summarises, 'is not historical accuracy, but a politically motivated need to insist on the contribution formulations of same-sex desire have made to Western civilisation'.[8]

Caravaggio holds a reputation as a troublemaker, a man said by his contemporaries to be 'a quarrelsome individual', and 'a pernicious poison who did a little good but much harm'.[9] Indeed, prominent queer theorist Leo Bersani makes purposefully anachronistic use of 20th-century *enfant terrible*

---

5   Elizabeth Freeman, *Time Binds: Queer Temporalities, Queer Histories* (Durham, NC and London: Duke University Press, 2010), xvi.

6   Derek Jarman, *At Your Own Risk: A Saint's Testament* (London: Vintage, 1992), 46.

7   *At Your Own Risk*, 46. For an account of the history of reclaiming the queer past through lists of queer forebears, see Gregory Woods, *A History of Gay Literature: The Male Tradition* (New Haven, CT: Yale University Press, 1998), 3–6. Woods traces the approach back to around 1870, to 'bookish homosexuals' (3) who were, for example, students of Walter Pater at Oxford. For a summary of scholarly interpretations of Caravaggio's sexuality, see Leo Bersani and Ulysse Dutoit, *Caravaggio's Secrets* (Cambridge, MA: MIT Press, 2001), 9–11. Bersani and Dutoit point out the tendentious nature of some of the early criticism advocating for Caravaggio's homosexuality, especially Donald Posner's essay, 'Caravaggio's homo-erotic early works', *Art Quarterly*, 34 (1971): 301–24; and Michael Kitson, *The Complete Paintings of Caravaggio* (New York: Harry N. Abrams, 1967). They note that 'distinguished scholar Howard Hibbard remains sensibly neutral on the subject' (Bersani and Dutoit, *Caravaggio's Secrets*, 10). Further accounts can be found in Ellis, *Derek Jarman's Angelic Conversations*, 114; Andrew Graham-Dixon, *Caravaggio: A Life Sacred and Profane* (London: Penguin, 2011), 4.

8   Pascale Aebischer, *Screening Early Modern Drama: Beyond Shakespeare* (Cambridge and New York: Cambridge University Press, 2013), 30–1.

9   Quoted in Jarman, *Derek Jarman's Caravaggio: The Complete Film Script and Commentaries* (London: Thames & Hudson, 1986), 44 (Baglione), 58 (unattributed).

Jean Genet, branding Caravaggio 'that Genet-type outlaw', in an essay that, in its investment in queering temporality, could be said to continue Jarman's own queer history project.[10] Jarman makes plain his interest in the painter in *Derek Jarman's Caravaggio*: 'Caravaggio was the first to take a bottle of paint-stripper to the Renaissance. He burnt away decorum and the ideal, splattered the clear clean colours of Mannerism with his lamp-blacks, knocked the saints out of the sky and onto the streets, stole and smelted their haloes.'[11] Jarman names a technique here that also became his own: he too 'take[s] a bottle of paint-stripper' to his subject matter, paring it back to its base components in order to make something direct and useful in his contemporary moment. Genevieve Warwick explains that Caravaggio 'conceived of his subject as a performance of history staged in the present. [...] Caravaggio demonstrated the relevance of the past to his contemporaries by enacting it within the framework of the present.'[12] Jarman shares his approach to the past with the painter. Jim Ellis links Jarman's technique to the artist's: 'Jarman figures Caravaggio in the same way that Caravaggio remakes his historical subjects, making them embody the relation between two historical moments.'[13] When Jarman writes 'I am obsessed by the interpretation of the past', in *Derek Jarman's Caravaggio*, he is pointing to his preoccupation not with the past itself, but with its 'interpretation' or, in other words, it is the past as seen through the lens of the present that provides illumination through its combination.[14]

Caravaggio's self-representations: *Bacchino Malato*

As well as finding in Caravaggio a way of working with the past that he admired and at times emulated, Jarman was preoccupied with Caravaggio's self-representations. The artist's self-portraits often use mythmaking strategies that bear further analysis because they were taken up by Jarman in his own work. Caravaggio's work was often highly self-referential: he would sometimes give his own features to a character in the religious or classical scenes and, like Jarman, would generally work with a group of collaborators who modelled for him and were involved in his own life. These methods ensured his painting acted as a kind of autobiographical practice or, as David Stone contends, show him to have created a 'mythical self [...] which critics have often mistaken for autobiography'.[15] Like Jarman, Caravaggio demands

10 Leo Bersani, 'Is there a gay art?', in *Is the Rectum a Grave?: And Other Essays* (Chicago, IL: University of Chicago Press, 2009), 31–5 (35).

11 *Derek Jarman's Caravaggio*, 44.

12 'Introduction', *Caravaggio: Realism, Rebellion, Reception*, ed. Genevieve Warwick (Newark, DE: University of Delaware Press, 2006), 13–22 (19).

13 Ellis, *Derek Jarman's Angelic Conversations*, 117.

14 *Derek Jarman's Caravaggio*, 44.

15 David Stone, 'Self and myth in Caravaggio's "David and Goliath"', in *Caravaggio: Realis Rebellion, Reception*, ed. Warwick, 36–46 (36).

Figure 2.1. Spread from Derek Jarman's Caravaggio *showing the young Caravaggio (Dexter Fletcher) in a hospital bed, with the* Bacchino Malato *resting on the wall behind him (verso). The script relating to the production shot is reproduced, along with a quotation from Giulio Mancini (1559–1630), whose* Considerazione *is one of the earliest sources for biographical information about Caravaggio. Caravaggio's* Bacchino Malato *(c. 1593–4) is also reproduced in black and white (recto). Photograph by Gerald Incandela (24–5).*

acknowledgement of the inseparability of life and art.

In an early self-portrait, Caravaggio uses his own boy-like features for his *Bacchino Malato*, or *Young Sick Bacchus* (c. 1593–4), the god of unrestrained consumption and ritual madness, sick with surfeit. Bersani reads the self-portrait as an 'erotic tease' which provides a 'come-on' tempered by ambiguity.[16] The young Caravaggio poses coyly: he wears an open expression on his face and his bare shoulder is enticingly angled towards the painting's viewers, yet his body is shrouded loosely in material and is facing away from viewers, in a gesture that 'is at once exhibitionist and self-concealing'.[17] The boy is also depicted with greenish skin, demonstrating his sickness, adding what Bersani and Dutoit describe as 'a repellent and repelling note to the provocation'.[18] The intriguing pose that Caravaggio takes on in this early painting offers viewers the opportunity to interpret it in tendentious ways: he becomes the vision of the onlooker's downfall, simultaneously revealing the initial attraction and ensuing catastrophe that will result if one gives in to one's urges. Yet he is an ambiguous character in another way: he trades

Bersani, 'Is there a gay art?' 35, Bersani and Dutoit, *Caravaggio's Secrets*, 3.

Bersani and Dutoit, *Caravaggio's Secrets*, 3.

ʾbid.

on an androgynous gender presentation to attract his disciples, providing an opportunity for a contemporary viewer to read the pose as a commentary on gender and sexuality. However, the Bacchus is a choreographed pose, which complicates the autobiographical significance of this work.

Jarman uses the painting as a plot device in *Caravaggio*, which he expands upon in *Derek Jarman's Caravaggio* (see figure 2.1). Early in Jarman's film, the older Michele states in a voiceover that 'I painted myself as Bacchus and took on his fate, a wild orgiastic dismemberment'.[19] Although the older man comments on the self-representation as being a role he took on, the younger Caravaggio is depicted as being fully invested in that role. In the same scene, a reproduction of *Bacchino Malato*, created by Christopher Hobbs, is shown leaning against a wall, prompting a discussion of the painting between the Cardinal Del Monte and the young Michele:

> DEL MONTE
> Why did you paint the flesh so green?
>
> MICHELE
> I've been ill all summer, Excellency.
> It's true to life.
>
> DEL MONTE
> And art?
>
> MICHELE
> It isn't art.[20]

Jarman here guides us to a particular interpretation of the self-portrait: while enacting the role of Bacchus as he poses for his own painting, the young artist becomes Bacchus. Or rather, Bacchus becomes the young artist: the real subject becomes indistinguishable from the mythic origins that inspired the painting. Although sources from this period are inconclusive, they agree that at one point as a young man, Caravaggio fell extremely ill and spent six months in the hospital of Santa Maria della Consolazione. This painting is, in part, an autobiographical record of the physical effects of the sickness. The scene is repeated in *Derek Jarman's Caravaggio*, though with Michele's last line altered to 'It doesn't pretend to be art', rather than the simpler 'It isn't art' of the film.[21] Jarman has Michele declare the painting's lack of 'preten[ce]', focusing on his interest in depicting life without regard for aesthetics, and his scorn for the practice of elevating life to art.[22] Of course, this could also be a pose, but it gives a good indication of how Jarman wishes us to understand Caravaggio's self-representational gesture here.

19   Derek Jarman, dir., *Caravaggio*, 1986, 00:10:42; script: *Derek Jarman's Caravaggio*, 21.
20   *Caravaggio*, 00:11:45–00:12:02.
21   *Derek Jarman's Caravaggio*, 25.
22   *Derek Jarman's Caravaggio*, 25.

Figure 2.2.
Cover image:
Derek Jarman's
Caravaggio. *The*
young Caravaggio
(Dexter Fletcher)
here grasps the
severed head of the
older Caravaggio
(Nigel Terry) in
Jarman's tableau.
Photograph by
Gerald Incandela.

Caravaggio's self-representations: *David with the Head of Goliath*

In a second major self-portrait, Caravaggio uses his own features to disquieting effect in a graphic depiction of the David and Goliath story. In one of his engagements with the biblical story, entitled *David with the Head of Goliath* (c. 1605–10) and held in the Galleria Borghese, Caravaggio paints his own features onto the dismembered head of the vanquished giant.[23] The intense drama of the scene in the painting is aided by the young David's stance: he holds Goliath's severed head by its hair, its blood pours from the torn flesh at its neck. There is a scholarly consensus that Goliath's features belong to Caravaggio, derived from a comparison of the painting with the famous portrait of Caravaggio by Ottavio Leoni (c. 1621). To a contemporary viewer, this self-depiction seems striking. Why would Caravaggio have used

---

23   I refer to the version held in the Galleria Borghese, Rome, formerly in the collection of Scipione Borghese. Caravaggio also painted two other versions: *David with the Head of Goliath* (1607) held in the Kunsthistorisches Museum, Vienna, and the early *David and Goliath* (c. 1599) held in the Prado, Madrid. Neither of these versions are self-portraits.

his own features on Goliath? To understand this pose, one might consider who he is depicting himself as being vanquished by. There are two competing readings that comment on the identity of David. In the first, David, whose expression contains more sadness than delight in conquering his adversary, betrays 'an unusual psychological bond' between the two.[24] The figure is thought to have the features of a former studio boy, Cecco del Caravaggio, 'il suo Caravaggino', who had been his lover.[25] In this version, one can read the painting as Caravaggio's statement of being slain by desire for the younger man. In the second interpretation of David's identity, his features are thought in fact to be Caravaggio's own, as a younger man. In this version, the double self-portrait of 'self-mutilation' perhaps indicates Caravaggio's acceptance that the behaviour of his youthful self has curtailed his life as a man.[26] In both versions, Caravaggio uses a familiar religious subject to reflect on his own life (and perhaps relationships).[27]

David Stone describes Caravaggio's self-portraits as 'demonstrations of the artist's fierce competitiveness and quest for originality'.[28] Yet his painting of his severed head in this instance has a curious parallel with the self-portraits of Michelangelo, who is also included in Jarman's list of queer Renaissance figures in *At Your Own Risk*. These are found in the Sistine Chapel frescoes which were made up to a century earlier (ceiling: 1508–12; *The Last Judgment*: 1536–41). Strikingly, Michelangelo uses his own features on the decapitated head of Holofernes in the *Judith and Holofernes* lunette on the Sistine ceiling, placing himself in the role of the lecherous Assyrian general whose desire for Judith was the weakness that led to his death: he allowed her to enter his tent while he was unguarded, whereupon she killed him before he could destroy the city of Bethulia, her home. In this role, Michelangelo becomes the warmonger destroyed by his own (heterosexual) lust. In a second, later self-portrait within the *Last Judgment*, Michelangelo again depicts himself in a mutilated form, this time as St Bartholemew's flayed skin, held by the saint as the symbol of his martyrdom in a pose Laura Camille Agoston describes as 'simultaneously self-aggrandizing and self-annihilating'.[29]

In the context of these examples from Michelangelo's work, Caravaggio's own grisly self-representational pose as Goliath does not seem extraordinary but, instead, an example of how he borrowed techniques not only from distant spiritual narratives and classical myth, but also from his more recent cultural history. Agoston has written at length about the convention in Italian

24 Catherine Puglisi, *Caravaggio* (London: Phaidon Press, 2000), 363.

25 Quoted in Puglisi, *Caravaggio*, 363. For an account of the gossip circulating throughout the 17th century and various unverifiable accounts, see Puglisi, *Caravaggio*, 363.

26 Stone, 'Self and myth', 41.

27 For an analysis of the painting as self-mutilation, see Stone, 'Self and myth', 41; Alfred Moir, *Caravaggio* (New York: Harry N. Abrams, 1989), 116.

28 Stone, 'Self and myth', 43.

29 Laura Camille Agoston, 'Sonnet, sculpture, death: the mediums of Michaelangelo's self-imaging', *Art History*, 20.4 (1997): 534–55 (546).

Renaissance and Baroque painting of artists making self-portraits where their features are placed onto the severed heads of Holofernes, Goliath or John the Baptist. She observes that 'the biblical narrative is coded with private, autobiographical significance, while the faces of Judith, David, or Salome also take on a specificity known only to the artist and his circle as portraits of former lovers'.[30] These narratives of inversion, where the weaker person (the smaller David, the female Judith or Salome) subdues the stronger, seem to depict the artist as the rightly defeated victim. Yet they are always ambiguous: they demonstrate the artist's power to transform myth and biblical narrative into personal history. By preserving references to one's life in paint, one can enact 'durable commemoration and oblique revenge'.[31]

Jarman takes up the ambiguous backstory to *David with the Head of Goliath* (1605–10) most visibly in the book *Caravaggio*, rather than the film. On the front cover of *Derek Jarman's Caravaggio*, a hybrid photograph with hand-painted areas shows Jarman's tableau recreation of the setting for Caravaggio's *David with the Head of Goliath* (see figure 2.2). In this version, Goliath has the features of Nigel Terry, the actor who plays Michele Caravaggio in the film. The teenager holding the head of the vanquished Goliath aloft is Dexter Fletcher, the actor who plays the young Caravaggio in the film. His younger self holds the older self's decapitated head aloft, as it drips blood. By placing a double self-portrait on the front cover of the book, Jarman frames the Caravaggio project with an image that explores Caravaggio's biography through the painter's own autobiographical project. In this case, Jarman privileges a reading where the painter depicts the actions of his younger self annihilating the older man.

Yet Jarman includes another version of the scene in the book. On a spread that focuses on Caravaggio's self-portraits, Jarman includes one of Gerald Incandela's photographs – this one another full-size photograph of *David with the Head of Goliath*, recreated as a *tableau vivant* (see figure 2.3).[32] In this version, the image captured is different from that of the cover. This time the young boy is not the young Caravaggio (played by Dexter Fletcher), but another adolescent boy. The photograph has, like the front cover, been partly painted over, the black watercolour paint giving the piece a dreamlike quality. Jarman's text on the opposite page is ambiguous: 'Six years before, when he painted *The Martyrdom of Saint Matthew*, he included his own self-portrait, staring wistfully over his shoulder at a beautiful naked youth. [...] This painting and *David with the Head of Goliath* – another self-portrait, in which a tough street boy holds Caravaggio's severed head – show martyrdom at the hands of youth.'[33]

30   Agoston, 'Sonnet, sculpture, death', 546.
31   Ibid., 548.
32   *Derek Jarman's Caravaggio*, 49.
33   Ibid., 48.

Gerald Incandela explains of the second photograph that, in the making of the film, it had preceded the image of Dexter Fletcher. One of the extras had caught his eye because he looked so much like a Caravaggio model, so Incandela photographed him in the role of David in Caravaggio's painting. Jarman loved the photograph, so he added a potential scene to the film, which Incandela photographed, but of course using Dexter Fletcher.[34]

In a way, it doesn't matter whether the 'youth' Jarman here refers to is the painter's younger self, or another young man. Both versions of the painting's sitters' identities coexist: Caravaggio's posed self-destruction, as well as his demise at the hands of a young lover. The variant tableaux provide a lens through which to understand not necessarily the events in the film but Jarman's understanding and engagement with Caravaggio's autobiographical play. Of course, here the variation has been suggested by Incandela, yet Jarman chose to include the initial photograph in the book. The effect is to show that Jarman engaged with multiple versions of Caravaggio's life: those readings encouraged by Caravaggio himself, his contemporaries in Italy, and his afterlives in cultural history.[35] His own reading allowed for multiple versions to coexist.

The inexact match between the contents of the film and those of the book shows us one way to understand Jarman's working practice. This example demonstrates that the book is not simply a printed illustration of the contents of the film. Instead, it is an extension of its subject matter that shows far more than stills from the set. It reveals other possibilities and roads not travelled, and the collaborative working processes that informed the film's direction. The project is not simply about the finished result when the film was released, although that was a huge relief after so many years' hiatus, but about the collaborative process of exploring, then reenacting, the painter's history.

Caravaggio, Christ and Jarman taking things further

Jarman engages with a further example of Caravaggio's self-portraiture. On the double-page spread dedicated to self-portraits in *Derek Jarman's Caravaggio*, he comments on another self-portrait, which is subtly featured in *The Martyrdom of Saint Matthew* (1599–1600), installed in the church of San Luigi dei Francesi, Rome. The famous painting features the saint being murdered by a soldier the king of Ethopia has sent, repayment for having rebuked the king for lusting after his own niece, a nun. The young soldier, or murderer, is situated at the centre of the image, his muscles made more prominent by the direction of the light on his unclothed body. As Jarman

---

34 Gerald Incandela in private correspondence with the author.

35 Psychological analyses from the 1970s of Caravaggio's self-portrait as Goliath (rather than as a double self-portrait) and as Medusa (both 1597) read a castration complex into the self-representations that involve decapitation. See, e.g., L. Schneider, 'Donatello and Caravaggio: the iconography of decapitation', *American Imago*, 33 (1976): 77–91.

describes him, 'A murderer, who [Caravaggio] has painted triumphantly'.[36] A face, again recognisable from the Ottavio Leoni portrait of Caravaggio, looks askance at the scene from the background, perhaps 'a saddened bystander' or, given a queer reading, a portrait of the artist throwing a backwards glance at the beautiful soldier, perhaps claiming a relation of unrequited desire.[37] Jarman gives a queer reading to the painting in his earlier autobiography, *Dancing Ledge*. He includes the following commentary on the painting: 'Michele gazes wistfully at the hero slaying the saint. It is a look no one can understand unless he has stood till 5 a.m. in a gay bar hoping to be fucked by that hero. The gaze of the passive homosexual at the object of his desire, he waits to be chosen, he cannot make the choice.'[38] The passage demonstrates the direct way Jarman makes a reading of the past in the terms of the present: the mention of the gay bar helps contextualise the onlooker's gaze, yet, once again, there is a hint of darker impulses than hedonism. Jarman recognises that 'it's difficult to know how the seventeenth century understood physical homosexuality', but the point is not historical accuracy but instead recognising and drawing out a lineage of queer forebears.[39] In Jarman's film, Ranuccio (Sean Bean) poses as Saint Matthew's killer in the tableau for the painting. Jarman thereby invites us to understand the painting in terms of Michele's unrequited passion for Ranuccio.

In *Derek Jarman's Caravaggio*, Jarman makes explicit his techniques in using Caravaggio's paintings as a framing device through which to construct a narrative of Caravaggio's life in his film. In the above example, Jarman makes clear his intent to use *The Martyrdom of Saint Matthew* to highlight the unequal desire between Caravaggio and Ranuccio. He names the implied relation in the tableau shown in the film. But in another spread in *Derek Jarman's Caravaggio* (60–1), Jarman goes further still by using Nigel Terry, the actor playing Caravaggio in the film, to extend the legend of the historical Caravaggio in a playful way. A grainy reproduction of Caravaggio's intense, voyeuristic *The Incredulity of Saint Thomas* (1601–2) depicts a religious scene following Christ's resurrection. According to the Gospel of St John, Christ appears to his disciples after his resurrection, and shows them his wounds to prove that he has truly risen from the dead. Saint Thomas was absent, yet when the others tell him they have seen Christ, he will not believe them. Saint Thomas is reported as saying, 'Except I shall see in his hands the print of the nails, and put my finger into the print of the nails, and thrust my hand into his side, I will not believe.'[40] Caravaggio's painting depicts the risen Christ forcing Saint Thomas to penetrate the wound on his side with a finger, as two other

36   *Derek Jarman's Caravaggio*, 48.
37   Stone, 'Self and myth', 43.
38   Derek Jarman, *Dancing Ledge* (London: Quartet Books, 1984), 22.
39   Ibid., 21.
40   John 20. 25.

Figure 2.3. Jarman includes another full-size photograph of David with the Head of Goliath in Derek Jarman's Caravaggio *in which the severed head of the older Caravaggio (Nigel Terry) is held aloft by a youth (49). Photograph by Gerald Incandela.*

Caravaggio as Goliath

apostles look on.[41] On the opposite page, a production shot from the film shows Caravaggio drawing Davide's hand towards him (Garry Cooper) to touch the wound on his side, the result of a knife fight with Ranuccio (Sean Bean), with whom he is in love (see figure 2.4).

Through this arrangement, Jarman places his reimagining of Caravaggio into a new self-representational role within one of his paintings. Jarman uses Caravaggio's painting as a framing device that helps him structure a film that looks to the art to provide a creative biography of the life. In this instance, Jarman provides a reading that extends Caravaggio's own self-myth-making: the character of Caravaggio in the film becomes a living enactment of the historical Caravaggio's painting. Jarman thereby places even more weight on a reading of Caravaggio's paintings as an autobiographical practice than

---

41 Reproduced in *Derek Jarman's Caravaggio*, 60.

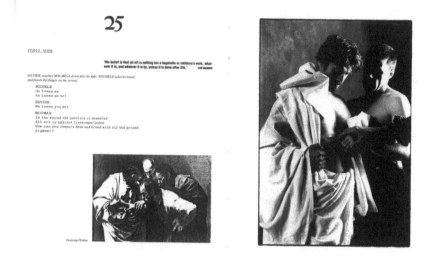

Figure 2.4. Spread from Derek Jarman's Caravaggio *showing a black-and-white reproduction of Caravaggio's* The Incredulity of Saint Thomas, *the relevant section from the script, and a quotation from Carel van Mander (1548–1606), art theoretician (verso). Jarman's recreation of* The Incredulity of Saint Thomas *is printed on the recto, in which Caravaggio (Nigel Terry) forces Davide's (Garry Cooper) hand into the wound on his side* (Derek Jarman's Caravaggio, *60–1). Photograph by Gerald Incandela.*

Caravaggio did. But he is also simultaneously doing something else: as well as commentating on practising life as art, Jarman is creating a symbolically resonant image. By depicting Caravaggio in a choreographed pose as the risen Christ, Jarman is depicting the painter in the role of queer martyr. Indeed, Jarman makes use of Christ at other moments in his work: this particular moment in Christ's Passion is a motif that is reprised in *The Garden* (1990), in which the older Christ figure (played by Roger Cook) opens his garments to display his wound to the camera, pointing to a history of gay suffering at the hands of homophobic persecution. *The Incredulity of Saint Thomas* is a painting that particularly lends itself to reappropriation by a gay audience: the original work is a startling erotic scene depicting an intense exchange involving penetration between men. By recreating the painting as a tableau in both *Caravaggio* and *Derek Jarman's Caravaggio*, Jarman, in Ellis's words, 'claims Caravaggio for a gay historical tradition, putting his sexuality at the center of his artistic genius'.[42]

42   Ellis, *Derek Jarman's Angelic Conversations,* 111.

Figure 2.5. Jarman in a cameo role as a cardinal in Caravaggio. *Production photograph by Gerald Incandela (*Derek Jarman's Caravaggio, *72).*

Jarman in *Caravaggio*

Another method Jarman uses to align himself with Caravaggio is the creation of an oblique self-portrait in the film, which is carefully documented in two richly coloured plates printed in *Derek Jarman's Caravaggio* (see figure 2.5). In what is Jarman's first physical appearance in one of his own feature-length films, he has a cameo role as a cardinal towards the end of *Caravaggio*, dressed in incarnadine robes. He is present and silent throughout the scene where a camp Pope Paul V (Jack Birkett) gives an audience to Michele Caravaggio.[43] They negotiate the painting of a portrait in exchange for the release of Ranuccio, who had been erroneously jailed for murdering the prostitute Lena (the real culprit was the pope's nephew, Scipione Borghese). The scene cuts to Jarman, who dips an aspergillum into a golden bowl full of water, then sprinkles it over some objects on a table. In the script, Jarman is mentioned in the scene's directions as follows: '*A cardinal takes a holy water sprinkler and silently blesses the immaculate paints and blank white canvas that have been prepared for the portrait sitting.*'[44] Jarman never looks at the camera or at the other characters but takes on a quiet and ritualistic role. The cameo in *Caravaggio* is brief and unobtrusive. An audience might not notice his appearance, taking place as it does in a tense scene between Michele and the pope. However, the fact that Incandela's images of Jarman posing as the silent cardinal are reproduced in *Derek Jarman's Caravaggio* in rich colour plates is a signal that Jarman wanted the self-representation to be remembered.

Jarman playfully demonstrates his own identification with Caravaggio through this indirect means: he uses the painter's own methods, mimicking the way Caravaggio used other figures to symbolise certain aspects of himself, rather than being more direct. By posing as a cardinal in the film, Jarman may have been gesturing towards his role as film director. The audience watches the cardinal undertake the almost spiritual preparation that underpins the making of a painting. Jarman ritualistically blesses the tools that will be used by the artist rather than seeking to show control of exactly what occurs. This mirrors Jarman's approach to filmmaking, in which the actors are encouraged to bring their own interpretation and autonomy onto the set. He places himself as an oblique observer who doesn't even look directly at the events taking place, rather than as part of the action, perhaps overdoing the sense of himself being at one remove from the action of the film.

Curiously, Jarman places himself in a role that notably does not involve a preoccupation with looking: Caravaggio's self-portraits always involve significant glances, as detailed above, and Jarman appears in other films in roles that always prioritise his ways of looking at his surroundings. For example, he frames his own role as director in *The Last of England* through repeated appearances wielding a movie camera, looking at the world within his film through the remove of the recording equipment. In the earlier film *Nighthawks* (dir. Ron Peck, 1978), Jarman has an extended cameo role in the background of a gay disco scene, where he leans languidly against a wall, casually smoking, handsome, observing the scene – in his own words, he makes 'a very creditable cruiser'.[45] In the cameo role in *Nighthawks*, Jarman remains at a distance from the action of the film: by looking, however, he is able to choose how and when to act, and with whom. Similarly, Jarman also

43   Depicted in *Derek Jarman's Caravaggio*, 120.
44   Ibid.
45   *Dancing Ledge*, 230. See Ron Peck, dir., *Nighthawks*, 1978, 00:27:25–00:29:15.

has a cameo role in *Prick Up Your Ears* (1987), Stephen Frears's biographical film about the life and violent death of Joe Orton and his relationship with Kenneth Halliwell, filmed not long after the release of *Caravaggio*. In it, Jarman briefly plays the part of his university friend, the artist Patrick Procktor, whom he knew from their time at the Slade School of Fine Art. As Procktor, Jarman paints a portrait of the naked Joe Orton for a commission undertaken in 1967 that would appear as a Royal Court programme insert. Again, he features in an observer's role: similar to the cardinal in *Caravaggio*, he is present during the film's action yet is not truly a part of it. As a painter in *Prick Up Your Ears*, he creates something new by looking carefully at his subject, but he tries to avoid being a subject himself.

In the cameos in Ron Peck's and Stephen Frears's films, Jarman is called on to represent an aspect of London's gay scene. In the first, he enacts an aspect of his own character: a hallmark of London's gay nightlife during a certain period, comfortably passing the time in bars, which the film's protagonist struggles to do. In the second, he is called on to represent London's gay art scene in late 1960s Islington by taking on the role of his friend Procktor. Yet in the *Caravaggio* cameo, a different kind of self-representation is seen: he is physically present for the exchange between the painter and the pope but demurs his role as witness to the scene. He appears to be presenting a quieter, more serious aspect of himself, perhaps reminiscent of his personality during his time as a student at King's College London. Here he makes a commentary on his roles as both painter and film director, and his identification with Caravaggio, as he blesses the means of artistic production. Yet more urgently, the role draws attention to Jarman's interest in temporal displacements, where several temporalities coexist at any given time. In this light, the self-representation shows Jarman in costume as part of the institution of the Catholic church, which has been so influential in justifying intolerance of and violence against queer people throughout history.

Jarman uses his cameos to point towards how the artist's body can act as witness, or as a reminder of the relation between subjects or even between temporalities. In a reading of Caravaggio's self-portraits, Bersani draws out the artist's use of his body as a 'relational term' in his art: 'The activity of Caravaggio's body in the work of his painting is figured in his painting by his occasional presence as a witness. [...] In this art, the communication of forms takes place, ultimately, as the artist's painted recognition of himself.'[46] Bersani focuses primarily on the work acting as a kind of mirror, bearing 'witness' to the events depicted in the paintings Caravaggio appears in, and to the act of painting itself. The movement of Caravaggio's body is recorded in the traces of paint he places on the canvas, but to ensure these traces cannot be misunderstood as somehow removed from the acts of the body that has made them, his body's presence is made yet more visible through the depiction of its likeness. Jarman echoes Caravaggio's interest in the 'communication of

---

46   Bersani, 'A conversation with Leo Bersani', in *Is the Rectum a Grave?*, 171–86 (186, 185–6).

forms' Bersani highlights by making his own body present in the events of the film, though at a remove from the action, underlining his identification with the painter.

Derek Jarman's project

Overall, Caravaggio shows himself to be a 'deft mythologiser of his own life' in the self-portraits I have detailed above, a description that Tony Peake uses of Jarman.[47] He takes on choreographed poses in his self-representations that mean they acquire myth-like properties. In *Bacchino Malato*, he makes a playful commentary on desire. In his self-portrait as Goliath, and perhaps as David too, he raises the events of his own life to the status of the biblical story, when posing as the vanquished lover. In *The Martyrdom of Saint Matthew* he becomes a bystander rather than a subject, perhaps making a playful comment on the purported role of the painter as an observer in translating ideas or events into art. Jarman demonstrates enthusiasm for Caravaggio's willingness to depict the body as fragmented, multiple, mutilated or sickening. In *The Martyrdom of Saint Matthew*, he even flirts with the body becoming irrelevant: an inconspicuous observer not tied to the action. Jarman borrows the technique of playing with ambiguity and inverted or perhaps unexpected power structures from the artist as a means of taking on historical narratives to speak to the present.

In an article subtitled 'Why Caravaggio's painting is even more exciting than his biography', Keith Christiansen, the Metropolitan Museum of Art's chairman of European painting, doesn't find much to love in Jarman's film. He states that Jarman has simply provided a useful introduction to some of the 'common assumptions' about the artist, whose 'impetuous, defiant, and often violent life has created a fascinating but distorting lens for the understanding of his works'.[48] He considers Jarman's portrayal to be a 'cliché' – 'Caravaggio as an archetype of the modern artist' – and understands the film as staging a clash between temporalities in its treatment of the interrelated nature of love (same-sex), violence and art: 'Rome circa 1595 meets New York circa 1985'.[49] His criticisms are valid only if one expects historically accurate instruction from viewing Jarman's treatment of Caravaggio. Likewise, Jarman's focus on Caravaggio's general reception makes him vulnerable to Christiansen's charge that the film is 'cliché[d]'. However, such judgmental terms are wide of the mark here: Christiansen's criticisms don't engage with Jarman's queer history-making as a means of intervening in the political debates of the early

47   Tony Peake, *Derek Jarman* (London: Little, Brown, 1999), 535. Matt Cook also explores the phrase in relation to Jarman in 'Wilde lives: Derek Jarman and the queer eighties', *Oscar Wilde and Modern Culture: The Making of a Legend*, ed. Joseph Bristow (Athens, OH: Ohio University Press, 2008), 285–304 (291).

48   Keith Christiansen, 'Low life, high art', *The New Republic*, 8 Dec. 2010, online <https://newrepublic.com/article/79749/life-art-paintings-carvaggio> [sic].

49   Ibid.

1980s and the vital need to create a queer past at a time when the future was anything but certain during the growing HIV/Aids crisis.

Jarman's engagement with the Caravaggio project is clear on this front. The book *Derek Jarman's Caravaggio* is a montage that emphasises the degree to which the film, like any other version of Caravaggio's life, is a construction. For Jarman, claiming a stake in Caravaggio's history by creating a portrait of the artist through his paintings in the film, then chronicling the interchangeable nature of Caravaggio's art and life in *Derek Jarman's Caravaggio*, is a means of claiming the painter for a queer lineage. Questions of historical accuracy may count to some extent, yet Jarman might respond that the queer content of much of the official record has been excised, so cannot be relied upon to provide a faithful account. He isn't seeking to provide a biographical film in *Caravaggio* per se, but instead to do queer work by laying claim to his sexuality through an engagement with his chaotic, violent life. As a result, his interest does focus on his homosexuality, and events in his life where his sexuality is closest to the surface. He uses Caravaggio very much from the standpoint of the then present: his interest lies in the *interpretation* of Caravaggio's life – and associated self-representations, not necessarily in the life itself. Where Keith Christiansen states that he sees 1985 New York in the film, his reading is surely far more of a compliment than he had intended. Ellis, whose work on Jarman focuses on his 'ongoing and shifting engagement with historical material', primarily from the early modern period, conceives of Jarman's entire oeuvre as a 'project of responding to the challenges of his own time'. He summarises an important point that I return to in this chapter: Jarman felt that by 'remaking the past, he was remaking the present, and allowing for the invention of new possibilities for living'.[50] Here, any differentiation or sequencing of the past and the present becomes less clear – making way instead for a queerer notion of time which relies less upon ideas of linearity or progress.

Although revisiting the past was a preoccupation for Jarman throughout his career, to do so did not always mean the same thing. Between the release of his first feature film *Sebastiane* and the release of *Caravaggio* and *Derek Jarman's Caravaggio*, the terrain had shifted. The making of *Caravaggio* came at a time when mainstream society's thinking about sexual minorities was rapidly changing in response to increasingly hysterical and homophobic media portrayals of HIV/Aids. A project conceived during a period of relative positivity finally came into being at a stark turning point. Although scholarly consensus is, as Ellis notes, that 'Caravaggio was his last work of art not to be marked in some way by the epidemic', this is not true to its contexts.[51] Its origins predate the epidemic, as do some of the script versions produced before its final form. However, it was filmed in 1985, so it is impossible to consider the work unmarked by its contexts simply because Jarman had

---

50   Ellis, *Derek Jarman's Angelic Conversations*, x, x–xi.
51   Ibid., 133.

delayed his own testing 'for as long as was decently possible' – until the end of the year of *Caravaggio*'s release.[52]

Instead, the double release of *Caravaggio* and *Derek Jarman's Caravaggio* marks a turning point in Jarman's career. For the first time, he made his working processes visible to his publics by publishing *Derek Jarman's Caravaggio* alongside the film, a technique he would use again to great effect in the later *Queer Edward II*.[53] The visibility includes making use of the traces of the process recorded in the large black sketchbooks Jarman kept throughout his career to produce this montage book. The newly visible approach makes clear his engagement in the process of making a particular work, rather than its finished product. Jarman privileges the energy and delight that come from the working process, claiming the process – the project – as the main point. I consider that Jarman's work here sees the process as indistinguishable from the final product, which includes the self-consciously visible marks of its creation. Jarman insists on Caravaggio as a model for what Dominique Viart calls 'the surrealist determination not to separate life from art, but to treat life as a work of art and vice versa'.[54] His detailed, recurrent engagement with Caravaggio's self-representations, and associated 'self-implication', marks the beginning of a new chapter in Jarman's investigation of queer histories in conversation with material from his own life. He insisted on the possibilities and uncertainties of queer temporalities as a means to unsettle and contest the politics of the contemporary that both threatened and circumscribed queer existence with increasing urgency as the 1980s wore on.

52 Derek Jarman, *Kicking the Pricks* (London: Vintage, 1996), 16.
53 For an analysis of the queer politics of *Queer Edward II*, see Alexandra Parsons, 'History, activism, and the queer child in Derek Jarman's *Queer Edward II* (1991)', *Shakespeare Bulletin*, 32.3 (2014): 413–28.
54 Dominique Viart, 'Programmes and projects in the contemporary literary field', *The Art of the Project: Projects and Experiments in Modern French Culture*, eds. Michael Sheringham and Johnnie Gratton (New York: Berghahn Books, 2005), 172–87 (177).

3. The queer art of Artists' Books: Hazard Press

Jeremy Dixon

Hazard Press is a queer, Welsh imprint that aims to create Artists' Books with individuality, compassion, humour and attention to detail. The term 'Artists' Book' usually refers to a publication that is seen as an artwork in its own right rather than as a book about art or a specific artist/s. I set up Hazard Press in 2010 after an inspirational visit to an Artists' Book fair organised by, and held at, Ffotogallery in Penarth, South Wales. This fair opened my eyes to the possibility that I could start up my own press because it made me realise I already possessed the subjects, knowledge, skills and means of production to make my own books without having to rely on an outside printer, or on the approval of a publisher, or of anyone else for that matter. I had already amassed a large collection of printed ephemera including postcards and cartes de visite, and I also had plenty of my own poetry to use as subject matter. I was also employed as a graphic designer and so knew about pagination, preparation of artwork and other tricks of the trade for readying books for printing. The fair also made me realise that I had been handmaking many different types of books (such as comics, scrapbooks and portfolios) for a really long time – stored in my attic were books I had produced as far back as primary school. I also had a ready-made name for the press; in using my middle name, Hazard (my paternal grandmother's maiden name) I reclaimed a part of my family heritage that bullies had seized on to mock me at school (this name-calling also formed part of the constant homophobic bullying I experienced every day).

Hazard Press titles do not follow the linear progression of a commercial print project. With minimal editorial, deadline or budget constraints, the books are much more freewheeling and intuitive, perhaps as a reaction to my background in the commercial world of graphic design. Encompassing the plurality of meanings of the word 'queer', Hazard Press books have rather unexpectedly developed into an ongoing project of autobiography based on poetry, memory, queerness, music, images, and a delight in the accidental forms and diversions that the journey of planning and making an Artists' Book can take. Over time the overall theme of the books has evolved to become more of a reflection of my life experience as a gay man. This realisation has, however, only really happened retrospectively and quite recently; it was not a planned approach for the press, although it can now consciously influence future titles. My creative practice is centred on personal history, research and exploration using chance and happenstance, recycling, different papers, colours and varying contents. I consciously produce only small runs, with an emphasis on the handmade, which incorporate evidence of human intervention. Collage plays an important role in the production of Hazard Press publications, whether by using found text or found images or by combining a variety of glues and print processes and bindings. The following two examples look in detail at the Hazard Press production process.

He Said Meet Me At the Fountain

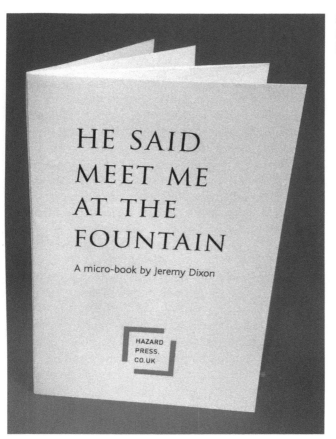

Figure 3.1. He Said Meet Me At the Fountain *cover.*

The book *He Said Meet Me At the Fountain* forms part of an ongoing series, which I collectively refer to as 'micro-books'. Each title follows the same basic design template and is made from a single sheet of A4 paper, cut and folded to form an eight-page publication. The micro-book could be regarded as the lighthearted Hazard Press equivalent of the mass-market Penguin paperback.

Figure 3.2. He Said Meet Me At the Fountain *centre spread.*

It is usually quick to conceive and execute, cheap to produce, and is based on images rather than words, a form of visual poem. *He Said Meet Me At the Fountain* was inspired by an early 20th-century photograph I bought from eBay showing a young man sitting at the edge of a fountain in the centre of which is a statue of an angel. The photograph was complemented by three other vintage images of men by fountains found online and a mock-up of the book was produced. However, I felt intuitively that something was missing and a slight delay in production and a fine-tuning of the content was required. One month later, the solution revealed itself when a counterpart to the first photograph appeared on the original seller's eBay site (definitely not listed there at the time the first image had been purchased). This new photograph was of a different man posing in almost the same spot and it seemed reasonable to assume that the two men swapped places to take shots of each other. This supposition is supported by the fact that both images feature a seated bystander in roughly the same position. After I shared the photographs on Facebook, an American friend identified the location as Bethesda Fountain (the Angel of the Waters) in Central Park, New York. The fountain was designed by Emma Stebbins in 1868 and has a prominent role in the play *Angels in America: A Gay Fantasia on National Themes*. This award-winning play by American playwright Tony Kushner was written in 1993 and deals with the outbreak of the Aids crisis in the mid-1980s. The second image now chimed with the rest to form a kind of pre-1960s image poem, hinting at gay desire, cruising, friendship, of secrets recorded on film, and of the calm before the oncoming storm. In the final layout the two friends at Bethesda Fountain are opposite each other in the centre pages, so when you shut the book they touch. The book has a queer content, but also a queer genesis, where luck and time and coincidence were allowed into the development process to enable the book to grow, rather than to be designed or made to a specific targeted brief, deadline or audience. The format of the micro-books means they are quick to make and cheap to reproduce, allowing them to be sold for a few pounds each, in keeping with the idea that an Artists' Book can also be a form of the democratic multiple. The series can also evolve over time: the content isn't fixed, and the most recent titles (*Tonight for the First Time Just About ½ Past Ten* and *So Here's My Number Call Me Maybe*) are inspired by lyrics taken from anthemic queer pop songs.

Figure 3.3. Collaging Ken & Joe *cover.*

Collaging Ken & Joe

Designed as a tribute to the playwright Joe Orton and his partner Kenneth Halliwell, the Hazard Press publication *Collaging Ken & Joe* mimics their London libraries collage subterfuge of the 1960s. The couple were arrested, fined and imprisoned (in separate gaols) for six months for stealing and causing malicious damage to books in Essex Road Library in Islington (coincidentally, I was born and lived as a child in Essex, an example of the kind of biographical connection that one often comes across). They would secretly remove books, collage image and text onto the covers and then return the radically altered volume to the bookshelves. Even at the time their prison sentence was considered particularly harsh and was perceived to result from all the homophobic media attention surrounding their case. The Hazard Press book contains a found poem, sourced from the interpretation and label texts that appeared alongside some of these original altered library books at the exhibition *Queer British Art 1861–1967*, held at Tate Britain in 2017. Each copy of the edition of 100 books has a unique collaged cover created from a full-page colour illustration taken from a water-damaged 1958 set of *The Book of Knowledge* encyclopaedias. *Collaging Ken & Joe* is a queer book, dedicated to queer forebears, which reflects its history and contents in its overall design. Unlike mass-produced books, each cover is unique, using a different image and cutout and with altered headlines to undermine the original meaning of

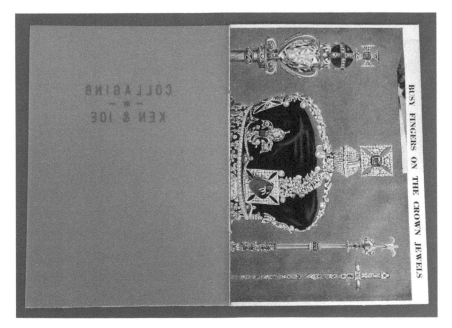

Figure 3.4. Collaging Ken & Joe *open.*

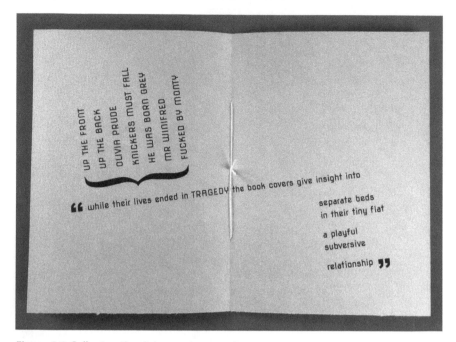

UP THE FRONT
UP THE BACK
OLIVIA PRUDE
KNICKERS MUST FALL
HE WAS BORN GREY
MR WINIFRED
FUCKED BY MONTY

❝ while their lives ended in TRAGEDY the book covers give insight into

separate beds
in their tiny flat

a playful
subversive

relationship ❞

Figure 3.5. Collaging Ken & Joe *centre spread.*

the colour plate by means of camp humour and/or surrealism. The production process does not follow the usual methods of book manufacture: the series of 100 books is being produced in batches of 25 copies; only 50 have been produced so far, and the rest will follow only once these books have been sold. The edition is also queer in that, unusually, the design isn't fixed and production is open to change over time. For example, its first 25 copies had the title handstamped on the back cover of the tracing-paper overlay, but after seeing the puzzled reaction of readers at a book fair – who didn't seem to understand just how the book worked or where to start reading from – I altered the design so that the title text is in a more traditional position on the front cover. This dialogue between reader and designer/publisher, which represents a blurring of the usual boundaries and enables readers to almost co-create future copies of the book through their feedback, could also be seen as another of the queer aspects that Hazard Press brings to the expected processes of book production.

I would argue that the production of my Artists' Books can be seen as different from, and also as subverting, some of the accepted norms of publishing, which in turn means they could be considered as an aspect of queerness, of otherness. Hazard Press is not driven by profit or the need to sell and does not have to work within any of the traditional editorial structures. The money raised through selling its output funds the production of future books, and I subsidise the press through part-time jobs and leading workshops and lecturing in colleges and at festivals. There is a non-traditional approach to content, print and production (in terms of recycling, different paper stocks, colours, small runs) and it is incredibly creatively freeing to know that I do not need to conform to any sort of hierarchy or to follow any corporate rules of design. Hazard Press titles are able to respond faster to events in the world and have a quicker production turnaround. It also means all the books are handmade, emotional and intuitive, a subversion of the usual means of publication. Artists' Books also allow for a queer means of distribution that circumnavigates the usual mainstream channels. Audiences can be reached without institutional or commercial consent through unconventional and more personal connections and networks, such as book and zine fairs, festivals, readings, independent and specialised bookshops, talks, workshops, exhibitions (all of which can be physical spaces but are also increasingly becoming online ones too), as well as through social media and the Hazard Press website.

I really hope that Hazard Press and the books I have made and will continue to make will inspire other people's (especially queer people's) creativity and confidence and help them see that they can develop and grow as a human being by producing their own art. In conclusion, I will reveal here the true raison d'être behind Hazard Press: I now see the whole project as one enormous FUCK YOU to anyone or any institution who has ever actively bullied, belittled, ignored, hindered or tried to deny my right to exist in this world as a queer artist, poet and human being. Hazard Press allows me to say I don't need gatekeepers, I don't need anyone's approval, I don't have to follow the usual rules, I can make my own way!

4. *Teleny*: a tale of two cities

Will Visconti

Teleny is credited with being one of the earliest English-language works explicitly addressing male homosexuality. It was written in the wake of other works such as Jack Saul's *Sins of the Cities of the Plain* (1881) and *A Marriage Below Zero* (1889), by Alan Dale (a pseudonym for Alfred Cohen),[1] and occupies a stylistic space between the two. Where *Sins of the Cities* was written by a male sex worker, it is a memoir or at least inspired by real events, while *Marriage* was fiction written by a heterosexual man and narrated by a heterosexual woman about two men in a relationship. Both works were written under noms de plume whereas *Teleny* was published anonymously.

Teleny (with the full title *Teleny, or the Reverse of the Medal: A Physiological Romance of To-day*) was written collaboratively by several authors, one of whom is believed to have been Oscar Wilde.[2] The veracity of this claim has been the subject of much debate in the century since its publication, and it has been extensively discussed whether or not, or to what extent, Wilde was involved in *Teleny*'s publication as author, editor or prime mover. He had an established professional relationship with the publishers responsible for the first editions in English and in French: Leonard Smithers, who published the first edition of the novel in 1893, and Charles Hirsch, who oversaw the publication of the French translation in 1934. Hirsch had previously procured material in French for Wilde, including books 'of a Socratic nature'.[3] In editions published non-anonymously over the last 50 or so years, Oscar Wilde is often

1   Anon. (attributed to Oscar Wilde et al.), *Teleny, or the Reverse of the Medal: A Physiological Romance of To-day*, 2 vols. (London: Cosmopoli, 1893); also see Jack Saul, *Sins of the Cities of the Plain; or, The Recollections of a Mary-Ann, with Short Essays on Sodomy and Tribadism* (London: privately printed [William Lazenby?], 1881); Alan Dale, *A Marriage Below Zero* (New York: G.W. Dillingham, 1889).

2   An argument can also be made for crossover between *Teleny* and one of Wilde's other works, *The Portrait of Mr W.H.* See William Cohen, *Sex Scandal: The Private Parts of Victorian Fiction* (Durham, NC, and London: Duke University Press, 1996), 192.

3   Anon., *Teleny, Étude physiologique. Traduit de l'anglais sur le manuscrit original révisé par l'auteur*, 2 vols. (Paris: privately printed, 1934); Robert Gray and Christopher Keep, '"An uninterrupted current": collaborative authorship and homoeroticism in *Teleny*', in *Literary Couplings: Writing Couples, Collaborators, and the Construction of Authorship*, eds. Marjorie Stone and Judith Thompson (Madison, WI: University of Wisconsin Press, 2007), 193–208 (194).

W. Visconti, '*Teleny*: a tale of two cities', in L. Kassir and R. Espley (eds.), *Queer Between the Covers: Histories of Queer Publishing and Publishing Queer Voices* (London: University of London Press, 2021), pp. 61–75. License: CC BY-NC-ND 4.0.

mentioned on the cover, either explicitly as author, or variously as 'attributed to Oscar Wilde', 'Oscar Wilde and others' and more.

The novel was first distributed in a limited run of 200 copies, with the events of the novel taking place in Paris. An anecdote recounted by Hirsch suggests that the manuscript was underway or completed as early as 1890 and in its first iteration was set in London.[4] When the novel was edited and translated into French in 1934, it was entitled *Teleny: Étude Physiologique* ('physiological study' rather than 'romance'). In this edition, the setting was switched back to London. The details of cities are not always given, with sparse references to specific landmarks or venues, another reason why the transposition was easier to achieve. An *avant-propos* was added to the narrative in Charles Hirsch's publication of the first French translation, excised from the English edition, he said, as was a further introduction.[5] John McRae's 1986 edition of *Teleny* 'restores' this prologue. The non-fiction introduction (a *Notice bibliographique*) tells of Hirsch meeting with Wilde in 1890, the occasion when the former claimed the manuscript was initially brought to him, and their subsequent acquaintance after Wilde's release from prison.[6] The delay between *Teleny*'s composition in 1890 and its publication by Leonard Smithers in 1893 raises the question of what else was contained in the 1890 version and its initial editing. The decades-long delay before the French translation is another mystery, but may be attributable to Hirsch seeking to capitalise on nostalgia for Wilde's writing, as a strategy to boost sales. More significantly, Hirsch's *Notice bibliographique* seems to vacillate between describing the author (not authors) as someone who could only be Wilde, while mentioning events that feature Wilde by name as if he was the sole author, at the same time as pondering the author's 'true' identity.[7] He poses the question of whether a clergyman was responsible, since there are religious references, or someone familiar with mythology because its classical allusions separate the work from other erotica of the period; or perhaps, he posits, the author is a family man with a wife and children, while drawing parallels to Wilde to pique curiosity in the novel. Certainly, Hirsch explicitly mentions the presence of Wilde's 'disciples' in his company, and it is these admirers who are broadly identified as collaborating on *Teleny*, thereby making it implicitly Wildean, if nothing else.

The novel's story is structured as a confession made by Camille Des Grieux to an unnamed friend and interlocutor, with numerous digressions into other memories or *mise-en-abîme* whereby Des Grieux includes tales, or stories

---

4   *Teleny: Étude Physiologique*, vol. 1, 5, 7; Colette Colligan, *A Publisher's Paradise: Expatriate Literary Culture in Paris, 1890–1960* (Amherst and Boston, MA: University of Massachusetts Press, 2013), 213.

5   *Teleny: Étude Physiologique*, vol. 1, 7, 9, 12.

6   Colligan, *A Publisher's Paradise*, 213; Rupert Croft-Cooke, *The Unrecorded Life of Oscar Wilde* (New York: W.H. Allen, 1972), 27. Croft-Cooke adds that the story was recounted to the publisher Maurice Girodias, himself responsible for a later French edition of *Teleny*.

7   *Teleny: Étude Physiologique*, vol. 1, 8.

within stories, which are told by characters within the primary narrative. The progression of the plot is also punctuated by Des Grieux's asides and questions or the interruptions of his companion. The *avant-propos* is presented as an episode where the same unnamed companion describes meeting Des Grieux close to his death, two years after the events of the novel, and explains how he came to record them.[8]

The plot details the lives of the young businessman Camille Des Grieux and the Hungarian pianist René Teleny, with whom the former falls in love while he performs at a charity benefit. Des Grieux, watching the recital with his mother, has an ecstatic visionary experience which he learns afterwards Teleny also shared, setting a precedent for episodes of sexual telepathy and out-of-body experiences between the two. Despite Teleny's involvement with and attraction to other characters during the novel, he and Des Grieux begin a passionate affair, punctuated with the latter's stories about his own sexual experiences and memories. These tales all feature women and are at best unsatisfactory, and at worst lead to fatalities. They include the attempted seduction of a maid, Catherine, which eventually leads to her suicide after another character rapes her, and a visit to a brothel where a woman dies of consumption. These episodes are constructed as a counterpoint to the transcendent love the men feel for each other. Along the way there are blackmail attempts, introductions to secret societies of men who have sex with men (some of whom are dressed as women), and eventually the discovery of Teleny having sex with Des Grieux's mother after she offers to pay his debts. Teleny eventually stabs himself – but with his dying breath the couple reconcile. In the prologue, it is explained that Des Grieux dies of tuberculosis shortly after Teleny's suicide, and the two lovers are buried together.[9]

The key elements of the novel discussed in this chapter are the influence on *Teleny* and its publication of the twin trends of Francophilia in Britain and Anglophilia in France, the laws around homosexuality at this time, and attitudes towards the Other. While the interplay of influences across the Channel was always significant, the longstanding rivalry between the two countries continued unabated. The to-and-fro of setting and publication reflect the ongoing 'culture wars' between France and England with pornography, literature and art at the heart of the matter, and the involvement of figures such as Prime Minister William Gladstone.[10] *Teleny*'s style and content cherry-pick from Wildean and French sources amidst classical and

---

8   See Oscar Wilde et al., *Teleny*, ed. John McRae (London: GMP Publishing, 1986), 191–2.

9   John McRae, 'Introduction', in ibid., 7–24 (12); Oscar Wilde [attributed], *Teleny: A Novel Attributed to Oscar Wilde*, ed. Winston Leyland (San Francisco, CA: Gay Sunshine Press, 1984), 22. Leyland is more explicit in identifying Wilde as the author. McRae's edition was among those seized during Operation Tiger, along with numerous other, less controversial publications. Other books were automatically deemed obscene because they were published by the Gay Sunshine Press.

10   Colligan, *A Publisher's Paradise*, 214.

biblical allusions, self-consciously trying to situate itself within a milieu and tradition of decadent writing at the same time as it explicitly positions itself as part of the emerging body of literature that addresses expressions of same-sex sexuality.

Publishing *Teleny*

Everything about *Teleny* and its creation remains uncertain and unreliable, from its authorship to its setting and its publication. In addition to there being no definitive authorial voice (or voices), the publisher, Cosmopoli, is fictional and remains difficult to pin down. This is because of the network of individuals, Leonard Smithers among them, who have been identified as potentially responsible for the creation of the first edition as much as aiding its distribution. A note on the inside cover of the 1893 edition, held in the University of British Columbia Library, includes Edward Avery and H.S. Nichols as potential publishers; Charles Carrington may be another. [11]

The first three editions were small, since after the 1893 edition, that of 1906 only consisted of 200 copies, and the 1934 French translation had a run of 300 copies. Divided into two volumes, the novel cost five guineas and was available via subscription.[12] When translated into French, the work was similarly sold in two volumes, available to members of the 'Ganymede Club', about which little is known beyond its name (alluding to the beautiful youth abducted by Zeus as a lover, who then became the god's cupbearer on Olympus).[13] The limited circulation of the book made it easier to remain discreet. So too did the subscription-only nature of its distribution, like its anonymous authorship, limited circulation and the fabricated publishing house. Moreover, the anonymity of the author(s) offered a degree of protection against legal action being taken on the grounds of obscenity.

Since the 1950s several single-volume editions have been published, in multiple languages besides French and English, as well as stage adaptations in Spanish, Italian and English. One of the most recent was a 2014 production of *Teleny*, staged in Melbourne, Australia. The dialogue draws directly from the novel, though the 2014 production made edits of its own, shifting the time period to the 1920s.[14] As with the urban setting, authorship and publishing of the novel, even the time period in which it is set has remained a slippery matter for scholars, since references in the text are not entirely congruous with each other, and mean that the story could take place any time between

11   James Nelson, *Publisher to the Decadents: Leonard Smithers in the Careers of Beardsley, Wilde, and Dowson* (Philadelphia, PA: Pennsylvania State University Press, 2000), 291.

12   McRae, *Teleny* intro., 8.

13   The term 'Ganymede' (*Catamitus* in Latin, the origin of the term 'catamite') also became a slang term in English and French for a homosexual, particularly a younger man.

14   Margaret Wieringa, 'Review: *Fly on the Wall Productions Presents TELENY*', 30 May 2014, online <https://theatrepress.com.au/2014/05/30/review-fly-on-the-wall-theatre-presents-teleny>.

roughly 1871 and 1891.[15]

As part of Operation Tiger, *Teleny* was among the novels seized during the raid carried out on Gay's the Word bookshop in 1984 (see chapter 6). The books were seized under a law implemented during the living memory of *Teleny's* first readers: the Customs Consolidation Act of 1876, rather than the 1959 Obscene Publications Act. Like other works seized, *Teleny* was accessible via the British Library and Senate House Library. In the British Library, copies of the first and subsequent editions of *Teleny*, including translations, are held in a separate collection of rare books since they are classified as pornography.

In terms of classification and genre, the novel contains elements of Gothic fiction and melodrama common in the 19th century, as well as the interweaving of ideas about the psychic phenomena that were popular at the time of publication. Explicit pornographic sequences also occur throughout the narrative. Historically, *Teleny's* publication is bookended by the Cleveland Street Scandal of 1889, when a number of men were implicated in a raid on a male brothel in central London, and by Oscar Wilde's arrest in 1895 for 'gross indecency'. This climate of anxiety about the exposure of one's private life pervades the story, as do questions of nature and sexuality, which subtly offer a challenge to the classification of same-sex attraction as unnatural and criminal.

The French translation does make some substantive changes to the English text; however, these do not affect the progression of the narrative. If anything, the Hirsch edition is tighter than the Smithers edition, because the digressions within digressions are trimmed, as are the asides about acquaintances or use of language. These are present to such an extent that even within the narrative, characters interrupt one another to stay on track.[16] In the digressions and quips lie the evidence of multiple hands at work on the novel, jockeying for control over a potentially unruly narrative and attempting to tie disparate threads together. At the same time the authors use the novel as a chance to showcase their erudition by means of populating the anecdotes with constant classical and religious allusions, and providing links to Uranian thought and literature of the same period.[17] While proving its mettle as a work of learned contributors, the novel does demonstrate awareness of the writings of sexologists like Havelock Ellis, and the argument for same-sex attraction being viewed as part of an august heritage with

---

15 McRae, *Teleny* intro., 12–13.

16 *Teleny*, vol. 2, 97, 112.

17 'Uranian' was a term coined before the widespread use of 'homosexual'. It refers to an intermediate sex as defined in the writings of Karl Heinrich Ulrichs, and was subsequently adopted by a coterie of English poets who constructed an idealised image of male same-sex desire or behaviour modelled on Ancient Greece. Wilde is recorded as using the term once in a letter to Robbie Ross, describing it as a 'noble' love. Oscar Wilde to Robbie Ross *c.* 18 Feb. 1898, quoted in *The Complete Letters of Oscar Wilde*, eds. Merlin Holland and Rupert Croft-Cooke (New York: Henry Holt, 2000), 1019.

precedents in antiquity.[18]

Part of *Teleny*'s positioning within literary traditions of same-sex attraction or decadence can be found in the publishing process, making links more explicit through cover art. The very printing of the first editions in French and English offers subtle physical suggestions of literary decadence through colour and decoration. The 1934 translation frames the text in purple printed borders on each page, a colour commonly used to represent decadence. Associations with literary decadence and queerness are established or reinforced through cover art of subsequent editions, as with the 1991 Laertes edition. On the cover is a still from the 1919 film *Anders als die Andern* (*Different from the Others*) featuring the actors Conrad Veidt and Reinhold Schünzel. The use of an image from the film – one of the first to address homosexuality but in a sympathetic manner – overlaps with other plot elements of *Teleny*, such as blackmail and suicide, as well as the prominence of music in the plots of both novel and film. The 1984 Gay Sunshine Press and 2010 edition within the Valancourt Classics series feature cover art which reproduces images by Wilhelm von Gloeden, famous for his homoerotic photographs during the late 19th and early 20th centuries, and who may have met Oscar Wilde during his travels in southern Italy. The earlier edition uses his photograph of a boy as the god Hypnos (with Wilde superimposed over his shoulder); the latter, a self-portrait of von Gloeden in 'orientalist' costume. Both of these connect to classical or orientalist motifs within the text. Beyond this, the alleged link to Oscar Wilde is used as equal parts marketing and literary continuity, with some editions showing his face on the cover.

Law and language between Britain and France

Legally speaking, there were a few key differences between France and Britain. Sodomy or homosexuality were not illegal in France, which explains rumours that several men fled to France in the wake of Wilde's trial in 1895 to avoid arrest or implication in similar scandals.[19] Wilde, too, moved to France following his release from Reading Gaol. French law had removed sodomy from the Penal Code in 1791. In practical terms, however, men who had sex with men still faced opprobrium.[20] This may have been another reason why the setting of *Teleny* was shifted from London to Paris, as a means of offering a marginally more forgiving setting, even though instances in France remained where men were faced with public scandal and their careers

---

18 See James Wilper, *Reconsidering the Emergence of the Gay Novel in English and German* (West Lafayette, OH: Purdue University Press, 2016).

19 John Cooper, 'Primary sources', *Oscar Wilde in America* blog, 13 Oct. 2015, online <https://oscarwildeinamerica.blog/2015/10/13/primary-sources/>.

20 Michael Kirby, 'The sodomy offence: England's least lovely criminal law export?', in *Human Rights, Sexual Orientation and Gender Identity in the Commonwealth: Struggles for Decriminalisation and Change*, eds. Corinne Lennox and Matthew Waites (London: Institute of Commonwealth Studies, 2013), 61–82 (64).

ruined.[21] Contemporaneous with the 1885 Labouchère Amendment and the Cleveland Street Scandal was the shift in other countries away from the persecution of same-sex-attracted individuals. In Italy, the Zanardelli Code decriminalised homosexuality, making the country a safer place to live, adding to its popularity as a destination for British travellers or expatriates seeking warmer climes.[22] Like France, however, homosexuality was no longer illegal but still not unreservedly accepted, and the attendance of Italian guests at the symposium in *Teleny* reminds the reader of the continued need for discretion.

When Britain's laws against pornography became more stringent in the second half of the 19th century, the links to France became stronger, and often material was sourced from across the Channel, another reason on a more practical level why the country, or more commonly Paris, was seen as rife with pornographers and as a hotbed of vice. There were networks between establishments like Hirsch's Librairie Parisienne, based on Coventry Street beside Leicester Square, and those in Paris. They dealt in the trade and publication of French-language works for the urbane Londoner, with sidelines in rare or pornographic material. These trade links extended to France, and to pornographers operating out of the Netherlands.[23] An equivalent establishment to the Librairie Parisienne was located on the Rue de Rivoli in Paris, and another close by, within the Palais-Royal in the centre of the city.[24] In London also shops used to line Holywell Street (since razed for the expansion of the Strand where the Gladstone Statue now stands). These included numerous pornographers.[25]

Within the decadent and aesthetic movements that rose to prominence in Europe (particularly in Britain and France) during the late 19th century, there are a few marked differences, and these should be considered in relation to the impact of these movements on novels like *Teleny*. The idea of transposing the narrative to Paris instead of London also has echoes of the censorship faced by Oscar Wilde in mounting his play *Salomé*. Its performance before paying audiences was banned in Britain on the grounds of a law prohibiting the representation of biblical figures, rather than objections to the interconnected narratives of sexual transgression of characters within Wilde's script. No such limits existed in Paris, where Wilde hoped to engage Sarah

---

21 Anon., 'Tribunaux', *Le Rappel*, 1 Jan. 1877, 3.

22 See Chiara Beccalossi, 'The "Italian Vice": male homosexuality and British tourism in southern Italy', in *Italian Sexualities Uncovered, 1789–1914*, eds. Valeria Babini, Chiara Beccalossi and Lucy Riall (London: Palgrave Macmillan, 2015), 185–206.

23 Colette Colligan, *Obscenity and Empire: England's Obscene Print Culture in the Nineteenth Century* (unpublished thesis, Queen's University, Kingston, Ont., 2002), 18.

24 Colette Colligan, '*Teleny*, the secret touch, and the media geography of the clandestine book trade (1880–1900)', in *Media, Technology, and Literature in the Nineteenth Century: Image, Sound, Touch*, ed. Margaret Linley (London: Routledge, 2016), 215–38 (225).

25 Lynda Nead, *Victorian Babylon: People, Streets, and Images in Nineteenth-Century London* (New Haven, CT and London: Yale University Press), 189–203.

Bernhardt in the lead role.[26] As a result, the original text of the play was in French and then translated. Stylistically, parallels have been drawn between some parts of the language in *Salomé* and *Teleny*, and the influence of the former has been argued as evidence of Wilde's involvement with the project. More likely, his writing had an impact on some of the men with whom he kept company, and the phrasing that evokes *Salomé* imitates his writing.

Aside from the translation between English and French, the novel employs a threefold process of translating language, nationality and space to both play with notions of alterity and transgression and to trade on perceptions of specific cultures. The translation of urban spaces as much as language offers glimpses of subculture within urban space, be it bohemian, queer subculture or hubs of sex work. When a group of men (Des Grieux and several heterosexual companions) visit a brothel, the Latin Quarter is reconfigured for French readers as 'the end of Tottenham Court Road' (ostensibly Soho) and identified as a space where sex work takes place.[27] Rather than bohemian Montmartre in English or the squalid East End in French, the choice of each district forms additional links to other texts. The Latin Quarter was likely inspired by Henri Murger's *Scènes de la vie de bohème*, and Giacomo Puccini's operetta inspired by the same text. Travelling to Soho during the same episode in the Hirsch edition reinforces Franco-English connections, given the district's long history as a French enclave. Conversely, when Des Grieux follows Briancourt and Teleny along the edge of the river through a space frequented by men cruising for sex, the 'Quai de ---' is left anonymous in French as *au quai*, beside the Thames. Elsewhere, parts of the city, such as bridges or the river that flows through it, are left nameless and suitably vague.[28] One element that remains in both editions is the fog enveloping the couple as they stand on a bridge. A vestige of the original edition when it was set in London, this remains in the Parisian setting despite having entered lore as the ubiquitous 'London fog' of Gothic, crime or period novels.[29]

In tandem with the vagueness of urban spaces is the deliberate choice of some characters' nationality, which remains consistent in both the English and French apart from Camille Des Grieux and the 'locals'. In *Teleny*, setting the male characters' queer sexuality at a remove by making them foreign diffuses a potential affront to the English *amour propre*, to quote Leonard Smithers, and also renders them more exotic.[30] Moreover, Teleny himself is

26   Will Visconti, 'The queerness of *Salomé*: putting the spotlight on Oscar Wilde's controversial one-act play', Senate House Library blog, 27 March 2018, online <https://www.senatehouselibrary. ac.uk/blog/queerness-salom%C3%A9-putting-spotlight-oscar-wildes-controversial-one-act-play>.

27   *Teleny: Étude Physiologique*, vol. 1, 70.

28   *Teleny*, vol. 2, 16; *Teleny: Étude Physiologique*, vol. 2, 12.

29   *Teleny*, vol. 2, 24, 33, 66.

30   *Teleny: Étude Physiologique*, vol. 1, 10; McRae, *Teleny* intro., 11; Colligan, *A Publisher's Paradise*, 213; Colette Colligan, *The Traffic in Obscenity from Byron to Beardsley: Sexuality and Exoticism in Nineteenth-Century Print Culture* (Basingstoke: Palgrave Macmillan, 2006), 215.

doubly othered. In both iterations of the novel he remains Hungarian, and he repeatedly speaks to Des Grieux in his mother tongue. Reference is made to 'Asiatic' or Romany heritage, enhancing the sense of alterity and possibly wildness.[31] When he speaks in Hungarian, the words are not written but rather described. Afterwards, a translation is given within the dialogue, as when he utters the phrase 'oh, friend! My heart doth yearn for thee!' His words are described by Des Grieux as being from 'an unknown tongue, so low and musical, that they almost seemed like a spell.[32] Just before the couple have sex for the first time, Teleny does the same thing, saying in 'a low tone, in that unknown, musical tongue, "my body hungereth for thee, soul of my soul, life of my life!"'[33]

Teleny's speech is also peppered with phrases from other languages, including Italian. Sometimes they are translated, but not always, which suggests that at least some of the idioms used were understood by the (limited) readership. The French translation minimises the use of other languages, particularly since Des Grieux repeatedly uses terminology like *merle* ('blackbird', deployed euphemistically instead of saying 'penis'). Such turns of phrase are often accompanied by asides to his listener ('as the Italians call it') that are excised in the Hirsch edition.[34] Phrases like *nouer l'aiguillette* ('tying the cord', a spell to induce impotence) appear in both editions, but without translation into English.[35]

In some passages the language is euphemistic and deliberately foreign, as if affecting a worldly voice mindful of the audience's delicate sensibilities, whereas other sections are much more explicitly worded. Still others veer from the poetically explicit to the bluntly technical, or the vaguely childish. This even applies to a section describing Des Grieux and Teleny having sex, in which the author jumbles words together, from the clinical 'glans' and Des Grieux's blood being changed into 'molten lead or scalding quicksilver', to the somewhat less delicate '[Teleny's] pointed tongue dart[ed] in the hole of my bum.[36] It is the hyperbolic and flowery turns of phrase that have lent weight to assertions of Wilde's involvement, given that some of the text can be compared to the rich descriptiveness of Wilde's language in *Salomé's* dialogue. The archaic phrasing is absent in the French, and some although not all of the more vulgar vocabulary is rendered more simply or clinically. *Anus* is used instead of 'bum', yet *verge* ('cock') appears in both versions.[37]

Some of the characters mentioned elsewhere are also doubly othered. At a symposium hosted by the aristocrat Briancourt, who harbours an unrequited love for Teleny, are two elegant-looking couples seen curled up together,

31 *Teleny*, vol. 1, 11–12, 32.
32 *Teleny*, vol. 1, 37.
33 *Teleny*, vol. 2, 40.
34 *Teleny*, vol. 1, 115–16.
35 *Teleny*, vol. 1, 123; *Teleny: Étude Physiologique*, vol. 1, 104–5.
36 *Teleny*, vol. 2, 37, 43, 56.
37 *Teleny: Étude Physiologique*, vol. 2, 24, 28.

whom Des Grieux identifies as two men with their female companions in fashionable dresses. When he remarks upon the beauty of the women in each couple, he is told that they are in fact all men. One of the two males dressed in a lady's *toilette* is an Italian marchese from one of the oldest families in Rome, according to Teleny.[38] This reinforces the othering of sexual transgression and its expression. Moreover, it feeds into the representation of the Italian male as effete or more likely to engage in homosexual activity. This too has an older precedent, with popular trends during the 18th century of *cicisbeismo*, or even potentially the representation of the *macaroni* as a foppish, dandified character as a precursor to the aesthete of the late 19th century.[39]

Similarly, the presence of the character Achmet, Briancourt's new lover, alludes to the popularity of orientalism alongside Anglophilia or Francophilia during the late 1800s. There are also colonial overtones, be they French or British, and assumptions about the deviant Other, particularly around same-sex sexuality in Middle Eastern countries. The writings of Sir Richard Burton and colonialist sexual fantasies featuring slavery and foreign bodies are also prominent in the literature of the late 1800s.[40] Briancourt is a dilettante painter, who uses Achmet as his model. Among Briancourt's works are religious pieces for which Achmet poses as John the Baptist.[41] Other connections between *Teleny* and *Salomé* are the presence of a character identified as Syrian and the inclusion of John the Baptist. In both cases, the role is filled by Achmet, who does not speak. The novel also expands the fetishisation of the orientalist Other across art, allusions to literature, and Achmet's public performance on Briancourt's arm. Moreover, Achmet is referred to as 'My Syrian' during the orgy he hosts.[42] The inclusion of orientalist motifs, including Teleny being identified as having 'Asiatic blood', provides an identity against which European culture can measure itself.[43] It also means that the space imagined for sexual experimentation is constructed as Other, but becomes a virtual space to conceive of sexuality beyond domestic confines for characters and readers alike.[44] The same applies to the Anglo-French division, with each being placed at a remove from the other in such a way as to defuse the 'threat' of transgressive behaviour by rendering it as a foreign rather than a local vice. Othering deviance extends from art to life, with the book traders who are

38 *Teleny*, vol. 2, 101.
39 Dominic Janes, 'Macaroni and sexuality in 18th-century', 25 Feb. 2017, online <https://brewminate.com/macaroni-and-sexuality-in-18th-century/>.
40 Colligan, *The Traffic in Obscenity from Byron to Beardsley*, 14.
41 *Teleny*, vol. 2, 90, 102.
42 Ibid., 90. The more general use of deliberately old-fashioned and formal language in *Teleny* (most noticeably words like 'quoth') could be an additional linguistic nod to *Salomé* and its formal, archaic phrasing.
43 *Teleny*, vol. 1, 32; Peter Stallybrass and Allon White, *The Politics and Poetics of Transgression* (Ithaca, NY: Cornell University Press, 1986), 5; Edward Said, *Orientalism* (New York: Vintage, 1979), 3, 7.
44 Gray and Keep, '"An uninterrupted current"', 197.

described as 'purveyors of filth' being explicitly identified mostly as Italian or French.[45]

In a discussion which crosses between French and English contexts, a consistent othering of vice with an entrenched cultural or linguistic precedent is observable. Like the earlier references to genitals, this serves as another example of how transgressive sex is inherently linked to foreignness, by no means limited to France and England. When talking about subjects such as condoms, venereal disease and sodomy, one country often blames another for what they describe as imported predilections. Consider that syphilis is described as the 'French sickness' in English and Italian while 'Frenchified' is a term for carrying venereal disease more broadly, or the othering of sexual practices. Sodomy is described as the 'French vice', and the French in turn attribute the 'vice' to the Germans or Florentines. In French, slang terms for condoms include *une capote anglaise* ('English coat', a joking reference to greatcoats worn by soldiers); in English they are 'French letters'.[46] The reason for the condom's nickname of the 'French letter' partially derives from the fact that they were sent from France, along with the traffic in contraband reading material, and posted across the Channel.[47]

The use of language around sex and profanity holds a dual function: it enhances the fashionable 'frisson of Frenchness', and thereby of difference and transgression that McRae mentions, at the same time as it self-censors by refraining from including swearing in English.[48] At the end of the brothel scene in the Latin Quarter, when a prostitute dies of consumption, the madame says 'la sale bougre', as if using French swear words offsets the shocking nature of the scene, or any of the novel's other goings-on. Then in the next sentence she calls the woman a slut.[49] During Briancourt's all-male orgy one of the men in attendance is given the title *maître des langues*. The use of 'tongues' has the same double meaning in the French and English languages, so the joke translates easily, but in keeping the French term for a teacher in the English text, the authors once more implicitly foreground French culture.[50] In this way, the inconsistency of the authors' vocabulary highlights the work of multiple hands on the manuscript, as does the fact that the text is a mixture of Gothic, romantic, melodramatic and erotic narrative threads.

45 Colligan, *Obscenity and Empire*, 8.

46 Michel Souvais, *Moi, La Goulue de Toulouse-Lautrec: Souvenirs de mon aïeule* (Paris: Publibook, 2008), 114, 194.

47 Colligan, *Obscenity and Empire*, 8; Therese Oneill, 'A dying syphilization: syphilis, the scourge of the Victorian sex worker', *The Whores of Yore*, 9 July 2017, online <https://www.thewhoresofyore.com/sex-history/a-dying-syphilization-syphilis-the-scourge-of-the-victorian-sex-worker-by-therese-oneill>.

48 McRae, *Teleny* intro., 11.

49 *Teleny*, vol. 1, 92.

50 *Teleny*, vol. 2, 119.

Literature and culture across the Channel

During the late 19th century, France was a key signifier to the British and to Wilde, but it was often a contradictory one. In English literature, France and the French language is perceived as 'sophisticated, urbane and decadent' at the same time as it is 'degenerate, self-indulgent and reprehensible'.[51] There also existed an image of France and French culture (that is, of Parisian culture) as an object of desire. This permeated all social classes, particularly in the wake of events such as the Exposition Universelle in 1889 – also the centenary of the French Revolution and the year the Eiffel Tower was opened – and the 1900 Exposition held in Paris, which Wilde visited. Paris was viewed as an idealised international capital, an arbiter of taste and a democratic paradise. For the English it was the simultaneous epitome of liberty, refinement and fashionable status.[52] Even the terms that Smithers uses in discussing the book are tinged with French, as a means of signposting associations with culture and refinement. When offering his account of *Teleny*'s composition and publication, he describes an 'eminent littérateur' (Wilde) who allegedly came to him with the manuscript.[53]

The spaces of same-sex sexuality were often also linked to culture, refinement and the demonstration of fashionable status in London and in Paris. Many of the spaces used by men to cruise for sex are similar in the two cities, such as theatres, nightspots and shopping arcades, including London's Burlington Arcade, and Paris's Passage de l'Opéra and Passage Jouffroy. Cruising spots at the less grand end of the spectrum include public urinals, known in Paris as *vespasiennes*.[54] Some spaces, like the shops and garden around the Palais-Royal, were centres for the pornographic book trade and also hubs for sex workers, male and female.[55]

While homosexuality was technically decriminalised in France, authors still tended to self-censor before their pages even reached editors and publishers, wary of putting their name to work that was explicitly queer. One example is Proust's short-story writing, from which he excised overtly queer content.[56]

51　William Cohen, *Queer Universality and the French Oscar Wilde* (Seminar presentation, Birkbeck Institute for the Humanities, London, 2 Dec 2009).

52　See H. Hazel Hahn, *Scenes of Parisian Modernity: Culture and Consumption in the Nineteenth Century* (New York: Palgrave Macmillan, 2009).

53　McRae, *Teleny* intro., 9.

54　William Peniston, 'Love and death in gay Paris: homosexuality and criminality in the 1870s', in *Homosexuality in Modern France* (New York: Oxford University Press, 1996), 128–45 (132); William Peniston, 'Pederasts, prostitutes and pickpockets in Paris of the 1870s', in *Homosexuality in French History and Culture*, eds. Jeffrey Merrick and Michael Sibalis (New York: Harrington Park Press, 2001), 169–87 (177).

55　Iwan Bloch, *Marquis de Sade: His Life and Works* (Amsterdam: Fredonia Books, 2002), 85; also see Michael Sibalis, 'The Palais-Royal and the homosexual subculture of nineteenth-century Paris', in *Homosexuality in French History and Culture*, eds. Merrick and Sibalis, 117–29.

56　See Finn Turner, '*I Do Not Speak French': Cruising, Magic, and Proust's Queer Sociability* (Unpublished thesis, Portland, OR: Portland State University, 2018).

Some of these stories have now been posthumously published.[57] Proust's writings are roughly contemporaneous with *Teleny*, and address some similar themes. Like Proust's *À la recherche du temps perdu*, the French translation of *Teleny* replaces the threat of arrest and explicit illegality with damage to one's reputation and social standing. In *Teleny*, the couple are sent blackmail letters; the same risk is present in *À la recherche du temps perdu*. Proust writes of the Duc de Châtellerault's anxiety when it is discovered he has sex with men after he crosses paths with a former partner at a party hosted by the other man's employer, the Princesse de Guermantes.[58] Also noteworthy is the Duc's use of English as a (failed) alias during their initial encounter.

Not only were there concurrent attitudes of approval and fascination, but there was cross-pollination of influences, be they conscious or not. In literature, performance and in language, 'the English aesthetes affected Gallicisms, the French aesthetes affected Anglicisms. *Teleny* is a meeting point of these aesthetic trends.'[59] The popular tradition among singers or dancers of giving themselves French stage names if they were English, and vice versa, to lend an air of cosmopolitanism or foreignness to their act, or to signpost linguistic ability and fashionable status, provides additional evidence of this. Parisian dancer Jane Avril is one example, as is Londoner Marie Lloyd.

The French references that populate *Teleny* indicate the vogue for French literature and culture among Anglophones, not just in relation to decadence or *décadence*, but more broadly. Camille Des Grieux's name, for instance, alludes to Manon Lescaut's lover, the Chevalier Des Grieux. Both Des Grieuxs outlive their lovers, and are drawn into their partner's financial difficulties. Manon Lescaut holds an additional layer of significance, like Huysmans' *À Rebours*, since both are read by the protagonist in *The Picture of Dorian Gray*.[60] *À Rebours* is identified as a text with a corrupting influence on Dorian, either for its content or simply its Frenchness, and it informs the 'urban sexual escapades' of both *Dorian Gray* and *Teleny*. At the same time, its influence is felt in descriptions and tastes in interior furnishings, settings and spaces described within the text.[61] In addition to Wilde's novella and Huysmans' writing, *Teleny* evokes Guy de Maupassant's *Bel-Ami* (in *Teleny*'s reliance on sex with women as currency), but also other works in English, such as the writings of John Addington Symonds. The connection to Symonds ties in

---

57   See Marcel Proust, *Le Mystérieux correspondant et autres nouvelles inédites*, ed. Luc Fraisse (Paris: Éditions de Fallois, 2019).

58   Marcel Proust, *À la recherche du temps perdu*, ed. Jean-Yves Tadié (Paris: Gallimard, 1987–9), vol. 3: *Sodom et Gomorrhe*, 35; William Carter, *Proust in Love* (London and New Haven, CT: Yale University Press, 2006), 181–2; Daniel Karlin, *Proust's English* (Oxford: Oxford University Press, 2008), 46–7.

59   McRae, *Teleny* intro., 11.

60   Oscar Wilde, *The Picture of Dorian Gray*, ed. James Gifford (Victoria: University of Victoria, 2011), 29, 89; Colligan, *A Publisher's Paradise*, 212.

61   Joseph Bristow, 'Remapping the sites of modern gay history: legal reform, medico-legal thought, homosexual scandal, erotic geography', *Journal of British Studies* 46 (2007): 116–42 (138).

with both *Teleny*'s publication history and Symonds's exaltation of same-sex sexuality, including references to classical literature or culture.

At the same time as combining genres and sources, *Teleny* sought to position itself clearly as allied to British aestheticism, which links back to the impact on it of *The Picture of Dorian Gray*. One can see glimpses of the rise in popularity of the aesthetic movement in how it is represented in literature, and the construction of identity during the fin-de-siècle. Des Grieux's fondness for majolica, while a marker of queerness, is linked to aestheticism via Oscar Wilde's quip that he hoped to be able to 'live up' to his blue china, and to the goal of aestheticism or decadentism as art for art's sake.[62] A taste for blue-and-white porcelain as a signifier of aestheticism or queerness is then presented as akin to the wearing of a green carnation, something apparently traced to Paris, rather than Britain, despite the novel *The Green Carnation* being written in English, and as a satire about Wilde and Alfred Douglas.[63] Wearing a green carnation was at one point attributed to Wilde as a trend. He admitted he was not responsible but expressed regret that this was the case.[64] The links between Oscar Wilde and porcelain also form part of the broader prevailing popularity of orientalism in interiors. The choice of specific flowers or porcelain is carried over into *The Picture of Dorian Gray*, but they are ambiguous since they have been identified as suggesting same-sex attraction or more simply aestheticism, as exemplified by the Peacock Room transplanted from the London residence of Frederick Richards Leyland to the Smithsonian Museum in Washington.

Where *Dorian Gray* is allusive in its references to same-sex activity, and *Teleny* is the story's counterpoint by making explicit everything that Wilde does not, there remain some curious silences. Despite the abundant references to classical same-sex intimacy and the opportunity for frank exploration of sexuality in an anonymous work, the same justification or philosophising cannot be found in *Teleny* as elsewhere in Uranian writing or sexological research. Des Grieux certainly alludes to what amounts to the view of sexuality that one was 'born this way', yet it lacks the intellectual engagement present in later texts like *Anders als die Andern* and Mae West's *The Drag*, which explicitly cite science and research on sexology by including figures like Magnus Hirschfeld himself.[65] There is no real philosophising or engagement with these ideas, however, which means that *Teleny* remains more closely allied to aesthetic or decadent literature by focusing on beauty, feeling, art and music rather than a scientifically or even philosophically based argument in support of same-sex attraction.

62 Richard Ellmann, *Oscar Wilde* (London: Hamish Hamilton, 1987), 43–4.

63 *Teleny*, vol. 1, 55; Matt Cook, "'A new city of friends": London and homosexuality in the 1890s', *History Workshop Journal* 56.1 (2003): 33–58 (36); also see Robert Hichens, *The Green Carnation* (New York: Appleton, 1894).

64 Dominic Janes, *Queering Desire* (Seminar presentation, Senate House, London, 11 May 2017).

65 See *Three Plays by Mae West*, ed. Lillian Schlissel (London: Nick Hern Books, 1997); Richard Oswald (dir.), *Anders als die Andern* (Richard Oswald-Film, Berlin, 1919).

Conclusion

The instability of the novel's setting speaks to the unstable and changing nature of the world as experienced by its characters through visions, flights of fancy, dreams and out-of-body moments, termed 'shared sensory synaesthesia' by Colette Colligan.[66] Similarly, the plot's unpredictability and intertextual references reflect the instability and sense of unease faced by its potential readership. The intertwining of Paris and London from the point of view of inspiration, influence and production are as much a reflection of the novel's composition at a nexus of creative movements as of the diverse foci and creative influences of the authors who composed *Teleny* in the first place. These authors seem to have been literary magpies, drawing on material found in other publications of the late 19th century in French and English, and most particularly from Oscar Wilde's oeuvre, while breaking new ground in the literary representation of unambiguously queer sexuality. By drawing on extant works to create heretofore unseen work that spans so many connected forms of transgression (across the sexual, spiritual and moral), the writers of *Teleny* offer a narrative that is queer in both its content and in its upturning of common modes of production or publication of literature through collaboration.

---

66   Colligan, '*Teleny*, the secret touch, and the media geography', 234.

5. Midwestern farmers' daughters: heartland values and cloaked resistance in the novels of Valerie Taylor

Jennifer Dentel

In their 1967 bibliography, *The Lesbian in Literature*, the editors of lesbian magazine *The Ladder* rated all known lesbian literature with A, B, C and T ratings. The first would indicate 'major Lesbian characters or action' whereas the last was a 'T for Trash'.[1] In their 1975 second edition, they cut out nearly three thousand 'Trash titles',[2] a large number of which were pulp novels from the 1950s and 1960s, the 'golden age' of lesbian pulps.[3] As a genre, most of these were written by men[4] for a predominantly heterosexual, male audience.[5] The novels were voyeuristic and titillating, typically featuring moralistic endings that fitted with traditional, heterosexual values. Lesbian characters were either vile seductresses who met untimely ends (usually by insanity or suicide), or naïve girls who realised by the end of the story that they truly belonged with a man.[6]

These categories closely mirrored sexological research that had divided homosexual behaviour into two categories: inverts and 'acquired inverts'. Seen through the lens of a common trope, lesbian schoolmistress and pupil, the seductive older schoolteacher could be seen as a pathological invert, whereas her younger, innocent conquest could merely be an 'acquired invert', one who had been led astray and could revert to heterosexuality once the

1   Gene Damon and Lee Stuart, *The Lesbian in Literature: A Bibliography* (San Francisco, CA: The Ladder, 1967). While A indicated 'major Lesbian characters, and/or action', B indicated 'minor Lesbian characters, and/or action', C specified 'latent, repressed Lesbianism or characters who can be so interpreted. This behavior is properly termed "variant" behavior', while T, of course, indicated 'that regardless of the quantity of Lesbian action or characters involved in the book, the quality is essentially poor, and the "T" is for trash'.

2   Gene Damon, Jan Watson and Robin Jordan, *The Lesbian in Literature: A Bibliography*, 2nd edn. (Reno, NV: The Ladder, 1975), 4.

3   Barbara Grier, 'Introduction', in Valerie Taylor, *Whisper Their Love* (Vancouver, BC: Arsenal Pulp Press, 2006).

4   Katherine V. Forrest, *Lesbian Pulp Fiction: The Sexually Intrepid World of Lesbian Paperback Novels 1950–1965* (San Francisco, CA: Cleis Press, 2005), xi.

5   Roberta Yusba, 'Twilight tales: lesbian pulps 1950–1960', *On Our Backs* 2 (1): 30–1, 43 (summer 1985).

6   Lillian Faderman, *Odd Girls and Twilight Lovers: A History of Lesbian Life in Twentieth-Century America* (New York: Penguin, 1991), 146–8.

invert's influence was removed. There were, however, several lesbian authors of pulp who managed to challenge and subvert the pulp formula. Valerie Taylor (1913–97), from the midwestern state of Illinois, was one of the most prolific, with her first lesbian novel *Whisper Their Love* (1957) selling two million copies and considered a historic milestone for realistically portraying lesbian lives.[7] Taylor's own life as an activist in Chicago clearly informs her novels, and they give an accurate picture of gay and lesbian life in that city in the 1950s and 1960s.

Early lesbian pulps could not be seen as promoting homosexuality,[8] and in order for them to be published, it was important that they have some sort of 'redeeming social value'.[9] Taylor herself refers in an interview to the standards expected: 'Apparently anything goes, just so everyone is miserable in the last chapter.'[10] Pulps, named after the cheap quality of paper on which they were printed, were often able to publish material that 'legitimate' publishers could not get past the censors.[11] Ann Bannon, 'the queen of lesbian pulp', argues that the status of the genre led to a kind of 'benign neglect [that] provided a much-needed veil behind which we writers could work in peace.'[12] Because pulps were disposable and low-brow, their exposés of deviant groups such as homosexuals could be fairly explicit – provided, of course, they left the reader with a moral lesson. While the blatant homophobia in many early lesbian pulps caused some scholars to view them with derision,[13] others, like activist Joan Nestle of the Lesbian Herstory Archives, have categorised them as survival literature. Buying one could be considered an act of resistance, often self-discovery, and one of few ways to find out about the larger gay community.

Within the pulp genre, pro-lesbian pulps could have a particularly large impact. Lesbian writer Katherine Forrest describes the feeling of finding an Ann Bannon pulp as 'it opened the door to my soul and told me who I was. It led me to other books that told me who some of us were, and how some of us live.'[14] Scholars such as Yvonne Keller argue that the pro-lesbian pulp subgenre was able to work within the pulp format to undermine 'oppressive structures by offering spaces, moments and even whole stories with incipiently

---

7   St Sukie de la Croix, *Chicago Whispers: A History of LGBT Chicago Before Stonewall* (Madison, WI: University of Wisconsin Press, 2012), 202.

8   Ibid., 147.

9   Faderman, *Odd Girls and Twilight Lovers*, 147.

10 Valerie Taylor, 'Five minority groups in relation to contemporary fiction', *Mattachine Review*, 7 (5): 13–22, at p. 14 (1961).

11 Yvonne Keller, 'Pulp politics: strategies of vision in pro-lesbian pulp novels, 1955–1965', in *The Queer Sixties* (New York: Routledge, 1999), 4.

12 Livia Tenzer and Jean Casella, publisher's foreword, *The Girls in 3-B* (New York: The Feminist Press, 2003), x.

13 Lillian Faderman, *Surpassing the Love of Men: Romantic Friendships and Love Between Women from the Renaissance to the Present* (New York: Quill, 1981), 355–6.

14 Forrest, *Lesbian Pulp Fiction*, ix.

pro-lesbian representation'.[15] These pro-lesbian pulps sharply contrast with the negative portrayals in most other lesbian pulps. Writers like Taylor consistently argue against social prejudice towards lesbians and provide positive representations.[16] While some argue it is going too far to speculate on the intentions behind these female pulp authors and 'few would suggest that they were undercover feminists seeking to subvert patriarchal culture by embedding radical messages in cheap popular novels',[17] a close reading of Valerie Taylor's early pulp novels does in fact appear to reveal this cloaked resistance. Taylor also speaks explicitly as an activist about her intentions to use the pulp medium to both educate heterosexuals and provide positive lesbian representations.

Valerie Taylor resented being thought of as merely a pulp novelist. Born in Illinois in 1913, she was a lifelong activist who began writing lesbian fiction because she 'thought that we should have some books about lesbians who acted like human beings'.[18] Her first novel, *Hired Hand,* is not a lesbian pulp, but it does include a passing reference to a character's early lesbian sexual experimentation. Additionally, *Hired Hand,* like nearly all of Taylor's subsequent novels, deals with controversial social issues such as abortion, sexual violence, gender inequality and poverty. Taylor used the profits from this novel to pay for her divorce from an abusive husband. She later lived in an artist community in Chicago, worked in publishing and wrote eight books between 1955 and 1965 while being actively involved in the city's burgeoning gay rights movement. Taylor is unique in that she was one of the first lesbian pulp authors to be relatively open about her sexuality. Scholar Katherine Forrest describes her as 'militantly active in the gay liberation movement'.[19]

As both an open lesbian and a political activist, Taylor is a unique author in the pulp genre. Taylor centres the Midwest in her novels and illustrates both the vibrancy of gay life and the beginnings of gay activism in Chicago in the late 1950s and early 1960s. Nearly all of Taylor's early novels are set in the Midwest, primarily in Chicago, with *Whisper Their Love* being the only work that primarily unfolds outside of that region. In the story of US queer history, the Midwest and Chicago are largely ignored in favour of San Francisco and New York. Even today, the 1969 Stonewall riots in New York often serve as the starting point for discussions of gay activism in the US, with much of the focus remaining on the country's coasts. However, the Midwest and Chicago have played a highly important role in queer history and the study of sexuality, with milestones such as the founding of the first US gay rights organisation,

---

15 Keller, 'Pulp politics', 17–18.
16 Claude J. Summers, *The Gay and Lesbian Literary Heritage: A Reader's Companion to the Writers and their Works from Antiquity to the Present* (New York: Henry Holt, 1995), 525.
17 Tenzer and Casella, publisher's foreword, *The Girls in 3-B,* ix.
18 Kate Brandt, *Happy Endings: Lesbian Writers Talk about their Lives and Work* (Tallahassee, FL: Naiad Press, 1993), 51–2.
19 Forrest, *Lesbian Pulp Fiction,* xi.

publication of Kinsey's groundbreaking studies of sexuality, and the launch of Naiad Press, the oldest lesbian publishing house, all occurring in this region.

Valerie Taylor was also a poet and political activist, involved in the founding of one of Chicago's earliest homophile organisations, Mattachine Midwest and the Lesbian Writers' Conference. This activism is apparent throughout her novels and, while they are still certainly pulps and share some of the issues found in the majority of lesbian pulps, she takes control of the genre and uses it to disseminate information to the queer community in Chicago, consistently challenging the standard.

Taylor differentiates herself by inserting references to books, spaces and terms to help illuminate the reality of the Chicago gay community. She also provides a critique of police entrapment and bar raids, the legal and psychological standing of homosexuals and, most importantly, she portrays her lesbian characters as distinctly human individuals. Without giving in to the voyeuristic tendencies of most lesbian pulps,[20] she hopes to portray her characters as 'people who [act] human, who [have] problems, and families, and allergies, and jobs, and so on.'[21] These women are sympathetic characters with chances at love, community and careers. While this seems minor, given the huge advancements in gay visibility and rights since the 1960s, positive representations of lesbians would both humanise this minority group for heterosexual readers and provide a lifeline for a lesbian audience. In this way, Valerie Taylor's early pulp novels subvert the typical lesbian pulp narrative by presenting resistance to traditional midwestern values as well as representing a growing gay community and activism in Chicago in the 1950s and 1960s.

Taylor's first and third lesbian pulp novels do show signs of having to adhere to moralistic publishing guidelines. In *Whisper Their Love,* the main character, Joyce, realises her lesbianism is simply a case of 'retarded development'. A helpful male character explains this to her and offers to have sex with her because, as he says, 'maybe a sample of the real thing would help straighten [her] out.'[22] He presses her by saying having sex with him would 'prove you're a normal female ... not tied down to something you've already outgrown.'[23] Somewhat implausibly, this argument moves Joyce, and she ends the novel planning to marry him. When interviewed in 1991, Taylor acknowledged that this ending 'was almost required [at that time]; either she [killed] herself ... or she fell in love with a man.'[24] In *Stranger on Lesbos* (1960), Frances, a housewife who has an affair with a female classmate named Bake, similarly realises that the lesbian liaison has harmed her family. She retreats to the comfort of her

---

20   Keller, 'Pulp politics', 1–25, cites Taylor as the paradigmatic example of a lesbian author who avoided voyeurism. Taylor 'successfully avoided sensationalism and extraneous sex scenes and worked to normalize, humanize and desensationalize the lesbian characters while keeping them central to each story', 6.

21   Brandt, *Happy Endings,* 52.

22   Valerie Taylor, *Whisper Their Love* (Greenwich, CT: Fawcett, 1957), 144.

23   Taylor, *Whisper Their Love,* 145.

24   Brandt, *Happy Endings,* 53.

husband, relinquishing any thought of future lesbian affairs. As she looks at him, she thinks 'what she saw was reassuring. What if he was getting a double chin? What if his hairline was beginning to recede? He was *Bill*. Dear, familiar, safe, the stuff of day-by-day living. After all, she admonished herself, life isn't made up of romance.'[25] These two novels, published in 1957 and 1960, are Taylor's only novels that end with her lesbian characters reverting to heterosexuality, and even a casual reader can observe the author does not view these as happy endings. In the case of Frances from *Stranger on Lesbos*, Taylor even gives her redemption and a truly happy ending with a woman in her later novel, *Return to Lesbos* (1963). While *Whisper Their Love* and *Stranger on Lesbos* do submit to the publishing standards of the time, Taylor still manages to insert subversive material within them as well as in her later, more pro-lesbian novels.

One key theme throughout all of Taylor's novels is the importance of books in finding community and educating oneself about homosexuality. In *Stranger on Lesbos*, Frances is encouraged to read D.H. Lawrence's *The Rainbow*, which leads to her lesbian awakening. In *The Girls in 3-B* (1959), Barby is given a lesbian book by her boss, Miss Gordon, with whom she eventually ends up in a relationship. After reading it, she is entranced and thinks, 'it was like stepping into a new world ... was it possible she belonged in that world, too?' This idea of books spurring self-discovery and revelation is echoed in *A World Without Men* (1963), when Kate spends the day in her neighbour Erika's apartment and examines her bookshelves to find titles such as *We Walk Alone*, *Whisper Their Love* (Taylor's own novel)[26] and *Edge of Twilight*. After Kate reads all day, Erika comes home and notes 'a certain lack of variety in [her] reading.' Kate responds that she has discovered something about herself through reading, to which Erika replies 'come to bed and I'll show you what you found out about yourself.'[27] Books, for Taylor's characters, are a window to another world and a chance to identify with others who hold similar feelings. In *Return to Lesbos*, which revisits Frances from *Stranger on Lesbos*, books are one of her only outlets while trapped in a loveless marriage to her husband. In describing the lesbian books she kept, Frances says,

> the book was one of those she had kept hidden in the attic, the boxful she hadn't been able to throw away even at the hour of her greatest determination to conform. She had put them away, promising herself that some day when she was brave enough she would take that box out and burn it. Now the contents seemed like a promise of better times to come. All those books 'in the field' – Bannon, Cory, Aldrich, Hall, Taylor, Wilhelm, Forster as well as the classics – said to her, 'you are not alone.' From time

25 Valerie Taylor, *Stranger on Lesbos* (London: New English Library, 1970), 107–8.

26 Brandt, *Happy Endings*, 58. Taylor acknowledged the in-joke of including her own book title within the novel with 'Yes, well, my books get a little inbred sometimes.'

27 Valerie Taylor, *A World Without Men* (Tallahassee, FL: Naiad Press, 1982), 50.

to time when she was safely alone in the house, she chose a title and plunged into the life she thought she had left behind forever.[28]

By inserting references to books by writers as diverse as D.H. Lawrence, Colette, Katherine Mansfield, Radclyffe Hall and other pulp authors, Taylor gives her audience resources for finding other places where they could find themselves represented. In an age where it could be extremely difficult to find any reference to gay people in books, let alone a positive one, Taylor is giving her readers a reading list. In a 1961 interview with the gay rights group Mattachine, Taylor acknowledged that fiction was a way to reach people who were ignorant of homosexuals. While most people would likely not buy a scientific textbook, 'they will spend 35 cents for a paperback with a lurid cover that they can read on the bus.'[29] Taylor even gives her audience locations of second-hand bookstores in Chicago so that they can track these titles down.[30] Taylor's choice to include real titles and authors is one of many ways she sheds light on further resources for her lesbian audience.

In the 1950s and 1960s, bars were among the few places in Chicago and elsewhere where gay people could socialise and find each other outside of parties in private homes. Taylor writes several fictional gay bars, from Karla's and The Gay Eighties in *Stranger on Lesbos* to The Spot and Happi Time in *Unlike Others* (1963). She also provides the bars' specific intersections and areas of Chicago. Taylor is essentially giving her readers an accurate queer roadmap of Chicago. While the names are fictitious,[31] the locations of these bars mirror the general sites[32] of many real gay bars in the Chicago of the 1950s and 1960s.[33] Taylor names general neighbourhoods[34] for her bars, and in *Unlike Others*, she even gives driving directions[35] that would have led her readers to one of Chicago's largest gay distr icts. In this time period, it could be really difficult to pinpoint the location of these gay spaces, unless you had a friend who could give you information. Taylor's books could ostensibly assist those who were alone and had not yet found their community.

In Taylor's novels, gay bars are sanctuaries where lesbian characters could be themselves. In *Return to Lesbos*, Frances observes a lesbian couple at Karla's Place and thinks, 'Here, at least, they could look their love and not be afraid of what outsiders would think.'[36] As Jo gets out of a cab by a bar called The Silver Spike, in *Unlike Others*, she anticipates, 'Maybe there'll be something

28   Valerie Taylor, *Return to Lesbos* (Tallahassee, FL: Naiad Press, 1982), 75.
29   Taylor, 'Five minority groups', 16.
30   Valerie Taylor, *Unlike Others* (New York, NY: Midwood Tower, 1963), 44.
31   *Out and Proud in Chicago*, ed. Tracy Baim (Chicago, IL: Surrey Books, 2008), 55–68.
32   *International Guild Guide 1965* (Washington, DC: Guild Book Service, 1965).
33   John D'Emilio, 'Rethinking queer history: or, Richard Nixon, gay liberationist', in *Out in Chicago: LGBT History at the Crossroads* (Chicago, IL: Chicago History Museum, 2011), 100.
34   Taylor, *Stranger on Lesbos*, 33, 98.
35   Taylor, *Unlike Others*, 105.
36   Taylor, *Return to Lesbos*, 9.

here for me. Maybe this time I'll meet somebody or learn something, and it will make all the difference.'[37] On entering the bar, her gay friend Richard remarks, 'Sometimes I understand why foreigners gang together so … this is like finding somebody who speaks my own language.'[38]

Although Taylor does portray many positive sides of the gay bar scene in Chicago, she is also critical. While the bars were places to find community, they were a limited option. Several of Taylor's characters, including *Stranger on Lesbos*'s Bake and *A World Without Men*'s Kate, are alcoholics. Many of her characters dislike the bar scene but view it as their only option for meeting people. Bars were also dangerous places due to the risk of public exposure. Taylor describes tourists who are 'out to get a great big thrill looking at the queers.'[39] In *Stranger on Lesbos*, Frances is recognised by a classmate who cruelly laughs at her and threatens to expose her.[40] Throughout her novels, Taylor stresses the harsh consequences of exposure. In *Whisper Their Love*, Edith's previous lover was a teacher who lost her job when she was exposed and then killed herself.[41] Taylor also exposes the problem of police raids in gay bars. Two of her novels feature bar raids and several of her other novels reference the ever-present fear when one is in a gay bar of being swept up in a raid.

In *Stranger on Lesbos*, Frances is taken to jail when police raid Karla's Place. This outs her to her husband, whom she has to call for bail money, and exposes very real problems for gay people in 1950s and 1960s Chicago. A prisoner at the jail says, 'They figure it's better to pay than get their names in the paper and maybe lose their jobs.'[42] When bars were raided, names were printed in the newspapers and people often did lose their jobs. Some even committed suicide.[43] In *Unlike Others*, Jo's friend Richard is at a gay bar called the Happi Time, when he accepts a proposition from a stranger who turns out to be a cop.[44] In this example, Taylor exposes the Chicago Police practice of entrapment, where male cops would pose as homosexuals and arrest men who took them up on offers of sex or companionship.[45] When discussing the concern that Richard's name would be printed, his friends ask what he does for a living and then reply 'could be worse. He could be a teacher.'[46] In 1964, shortly after the publication of *Unlike Others*, the Fun Lounge in Chicago was raided and more than a hundred people were arrested. While the newspaper could not print all of the names, they ensured that they printed the names of

---

37 Taylor, *Unlike Others*, 16.
38 Ibid., 16.
39 Taylor, *Stranger on Lesbos*, 36.
40 Ibid., 36.
41 Taylor, *Whisper Their Love*, 63.
42 Taylor, *Stranger on Lesbos*, 53.
43 Baim, *Out and Proud in Chicago*, 65.
44 Taylor, *Unlike Others*, 119.
45 D'Emilio, 'Rethinking queer history', 101.
46 Taylor, *Unlike Others*, 120.

the eight teachers who were arrested. The charges were dropped one month later, but the consequences of having had their names printed made this correction largely irrelevant.[47]

Valerie Taylor reveals great empathy with the different struggles gay men and women faced, commenting on the greater violence and risk of arrest to which gay men were subjected. In *Return to Lesbos* a character comments, 'it's lucky we don't have as much trouble as the boys – if a boy looks the least bit swishy he's had it, even if they can't prove anything.'[48] In *Unlike Others*, Jo worries about police raids but mentions, 'she had never heard of a gay girl being entrapped by a policewoman as men often were by detectives.'[49] Jo asks her friend why men are targeted instead of women. Her friend replies 'A lot of people don't even know women do these things.'[50] As with all these so-called benefits of being a lesbian rather than a gay man, there is a catch, with lesbianism being taken less seriously and often with an assumption, as Taylor espouses in *Whisper Their Love* and *Stranger on Lesbos*, that lesbians are just in a stage of 'retarded development' and will eventually outgrow it and end up with a kindly male character or return to their husband.

In *Unlike Others*, Jo bemoans how hard it is to find people outside of the bar scene. She runs through a list of ways to find others, including carrying a book with lesbian content or reading 'one of the special magazines.'[51] This reference to magazines hints at the growing number of activist groups, or homophile organisations as they were called in the United States. In the early 1960s, gay activism was growing in several major cities through homophile organisations such as Mattachine and Daughters of Bilitis.[52] Taylor herself was a member of both,[53] and was likely involved in two early Mattachine chapters in Chicago from 1954 to 1957 and between 1959 and 1962. She also helped to found Mattachine Midwest in 1965, an extremely influential group that fought for gay rights in Chicago for more than 20 years.[54] In *Return to Lesbos*, Taylor's character describes a gay activist meeting as 'a group for people like us. We have speakers and book reviews – like what are our legal rights and how can we get better jobs.' They have a national magazine and market themselves as a good way to meet people. The character later goes on to say, 'The last young man Vince asked was so disappointed. He expected orgies. We're very serious.'[55]

47   Baim, *Out and Proud in Chicago*, 62.
48   Taylor, *Return to Lesbos*, 10.
49   Taylor, *Unlike Others*, 86.
50   Ibid., 121–2.
51   Ibid., 86.
52   John D. Poling, *Mattachine Midwest: History of a Chicago Gay Rights Organization, 1965 to 1986* (master's thesis, Illinois State University, 2002), 17–32.
53   Brandt, *Happy Endings*, 57.
54   Poling, *Mattachine Midwest*, 37.
55   Taylor, *Return to Lesbos*, 63.

The meeting is nearly identical to the early gatherings of real US homophile organisations, and Taylor even admitted the group was directly modelled on Mattachine.[56] In the novel, the group invites a speaker from the American Civil Liberties Union to speak with them about their legal rights.[57] Similarly, early Chicago Mattachine meetings organised speakers to discuss legal rights for homosexuals. Homophile groups also offered opportunities to socialise. As Erika in the novel expresses, 'It is nice to sit and drink coffee with people who know what you are, that's all.'[58] Taylor's characters express hope for an alternative to the bar scene. She thinks, 'This might be one way to an answer – an organization, a magazine. For lonely girls in small towns, in colleges, in impersonal cities, at least the reassurance that there were others.'[59]

Psychiatrists are also common speakers at these homophile meetings. Taylor discusses psychiatry and statistics throughout her novels. While later activists were critical of organisations like Mattachine for their emphasis on assimilation and approval from authorities, such as psychiatrists or the police, this was an important part of this early movement for gay rights. The lesbians in Taylor's novels come across several psychiatrists and authority figures. Some are negative but a few are really positive. On the negative side, in several cases Taylor describes an ex of a lesbian character going to an analyst 'to be cured'. She discusses various psychiatric theories, such as lesbianism being a sickness or a case of 'retarded development', representing the mainstream psychological beliefs of the time. In *Stranger on Lesbos*, Frances's son catches her after a night at a lesbian bar and is concerned about the damage his mother's behaviour will have on his upcoming marriage, arguing 'Maybe this is some kind of neurosis you've got. Okay, go and see a psychiatrist if you think it would do any good. Only for God's sake don't spoil my whole life!'[60] However, Taylor's characters challenge these beliefs. In *Unlike Others* Jo explains to her gay friend Richard that one of her ex-lovers is seeing an analyst who thinks she is making progress. Richard remarks, 'Sure, we're neurotic. Who in hell isn't? Society breeds neurosis. I suppose the heteros who run around laying every female they can get their hands on are normal. I suppose the morons who rape and dismember little girls are mature mentally. Also the frigid housewives who are always so tired when their husbands come to bed.'[61] By ridiculing a psychiatric view that places homosexuals in the same category as child murderers and rapists, Taylor asks her readers to question their own views.

Though some of the psychiatric references in her novels are quite negative, Taylor also writes several supportive authority figures that corroborate her

---

56   Brandt, *Happy Endings*, 56–7.
57   Taylor, *Return to Lesbos*, 79.
58   Ibid., 63.
59   Ibid., 64–5.
60   Taylor, *Stranger on Lesbos*, 89.
61   Taylor, *Unlike Others*, 17.

lesbian characters' resistance to compulsory heterosexuality, including a minister in *Return to Lesbos* and a psychiatrist in *A World Without Men*. In the latter, Kate returns to her psychiatrist Dr Liebermann expecting him to try to 'cure' her of her lesbianism. Dr Liebermann responds,

> 'Not if you're happy. People have some strange ideas about this love business … As if we wanted to make everybody alike. As if the medical books had a blueprint labelled "normal" and everyone must look like it. I've lived sixty-five years, Katie, I've seen 'em come and I've seen 'em go, and I've never yet seen a normal person. Not one.'[62]

Dr Liebermann supports Kate's lesbian relationship and when she asks him if he thinks there is something wrong with her, he replies, 'If you love someone, you're lucky. The world is full of lonesome people.'[63] In *Return to Lesbos*, Frances seeks out a minister in a moment of desperation. Struggling to explain her problem, she finally confesses to him that she's a lesbian. Flippantly, the minister says 'What am I supposed to do, drop dead?'[64] He then goes on to explain that a tenth of women in the US are homosexual and how he is not shocked by it. He supports Frances's decision to leave her husband for a woman saying, 'then why are you asking me? You really have it all worked out in your mind … you have to find your own courage.'[65] Frances's relief is evident as she thanks the minister for not thinking she's a case of 'retarded development' and continues, 'Straight people almost never realize what seems abnormal to them might be perfectly normal to someone else.'[66] You can see Taylor's perspective through her characters' views, and it is interesting that she chooses these male authority figures to deliver a logical, reasoned defence of homosexuality. Perhaps Taylor felt these figures would have more impact on readers unfamiliar with homosexuality and trained to believe patriarchal authority figures. Pondering why the minister helped her embrace her lesbianism, Frances thinks, 'I only needed someone to tell me what I knew all along. Someone I could respect. Nothing was changed, but she went home full of new hope.'[67]

Taylor's characters find many sources of community, including the aforementioned bars, books and organisations. In addition to representing the public side of the homosexual community in Chicago, Taylor's depiction of private lesbian relationships is empathetic without being voyeuristic. Taylor's portrayal of positive lesbian relationships and domesticity is striking and contrasts with her often-damning portrayal of heterosexuality. *The Girls in 3-B*, which follows three roommates who move to Chicago together, provides

62 Taylor, *A World Without Men*, 156.
63 Ibid., 157.
64 Taylor, *Return to Lesbos*, 116.
65 Ibid., 118.
66 Ibid., 119.
67 Ibid., 119.

an especially good contrast. While Barby ends up in a protective, loving relationship living with a woman, her two roommates, Annice and Pat, fare quite differently with their male counterparts. For Annice, her relationship with Alan, a truly reprehensible character who abandons her after she becomes pregnant from coerced unprotected sex, offers a window into the misogynistic, racist side of Beat culture. The third roommate, Pat, provides a critique of the gender imbalance in the workplace. As the story progresses, Pat realises, 'it was evident that most of the problems and woes of the female sex grew out of their preoccupation with men.'[68]

Taylor's novels portray lesbian relationships positively with just a few exceptions. In *A World Without Men*, Erika helps Kate overcome her alcoholism, making Kate feel 'safe and cared for.'[69] At the end of the novel, Kate tells Erika that she wants a marriage. Laughingly they speak of domestic issues: 'We'll have bills to pay and dishes to wash.'[70] In *Unlike Others*, Jo realises that 'she knew couples who had been together four, five, even six years, girls who seemed to be faithful to each other, who didn't drink too much, who paid their bills and went on vacations together and were concerned with the everlasting female business of making a home.'[71]

This representation of ordinary domesticity is important. In addition to providing positive representations, these depictions also humanised lesbians to readers unfamiliar with homosexuality. Taylor argues that 'for many people with conventional viewpoints, books are the only point of contact with the offbeat people.'[72] Moreover, 'if the truth about the homophile movement is ever to filter down to the general reading public, we need more books which begin with the idea that what's normal for you may not necessarily be normal for me and that our neighbor may be still another kind of person.'[73] Taylor stresses throughout her novels that gay people are everywhere, giving hope to readers in small towns and challenging the idea that places like New York's Greenwich Village were the only places to find other gay people. Pulps were one of the few places where lesbians could see themselves and their community represented.[74]

Several of Taylor's characters muse that lesbians must exist everywhere. In *A World Without Men*, Kate 'supposed there must be others, in small towns, on college campuses, everywhere.'[75] In *Return to Lesbos*, Frances describes many cities that have gay bars and her knowledge that 'everywhere you went … you found the "different" ones, ready to recognize and welcome

68 Taylor, *The Girls in 3-B*, 107.
69 Taylor, *A World Without Men*, 30.
70 Ibid., 187.
71 Taylor, *Unlike Others*, 129.
72 Taylor, 'Five minority groups', 22.
73 Ibid., 19.
74 Summers, *Gay and Lesbian Literary Heritage*, 75 and 525.
75 Taylor, *A World Without Men*, 48.

their own.'[76] Taylor is fond of inserting statistics into her novels, which likely came from sources such as the recently published Kinsey Report. In *Return to Lesbos*, Frances reflects on lesbianism, supposing that 'it happened now and then, in a country where one tenth of all women were supposed to be gay.'[77] These statistics undoubtedly helped Taylor's readers, as she said in an interview, 'feel reassured and comforted when they discover[ed] that their own hidden feelings and secret experiences are actually quite common and not universally condemned'.[78]

In *Unlike Others*, Jo thinks, 'I'm exactly like a thousand other girls, except I like making love to women instead of men. So what? It's my own private business.'[79] This emphasis on private behaviour, and the assertion that a community of homosexuals existed, runs throughout Taylor's novels. The drive to find their people, whether it is other lesbians, gay male friends or sympathetic straight people, is often a driving force in Taylor's characters' lives. In Jo's fury at Richard's arrest she thinks:

> This big, patient, generous man with the compassionate heart and open hand, a lawbreaker. But that's because the laws are stupid … Any relationship between consenting adults is their own affair, but the law doesn't admit that, the law reaches into the most delicate and meaningful human relations with a big dirty hand and kills everything that's good.

Taylor's stance on private morality is clear, and she often uses her characters to express her outrage at social prejudice against gay people in Chicago.

In Taylor's early pulp novels, she manages to subvert the typical moralistic, anti-lesbian pulp formula by providing cloaked and overt resistance to the homophobic values that characterised American society in the 1950s and 1960s. Taylor inserts educational details with her references to additional books with lesbian content, as well as locations of gay bars and spaces in Chicago. She offers a glimpse of the burgeoning gay activist movement through her references to homophile organisations, and writes empathetic lesbian characters with generally positive relationships and aspirations. She consistently appeals to her readers to see the injustice in treating gay people differently, and the logic of allowing people to go about their personal lives in private. Taylor shows her readers proof of a lesbian world and provides resources for them to access it. Katherine Forrest, lesbian pulp scholar and author, argues that lesbian pulp showed lesbians they were not alone and that finding each other was the first step on the path to the gay civil rights

---

76   Taylor, *Return to Lesbos*, 64.
77   Ibid., 28.
78   Taylor, 'Five minority groups', 19.
79   Taylor, *Unlike Others*, 70.

movement.[80] To end with Taylor's words:

> We don't ask for propaganda, which is usually unrealistic in its own way and so dull that it defeats its own purpose. We do have a right to hope for books based on two civilized principles: That any relationship between two adults, entered into by mutual consent, is legitimate; and that any relationship that makes both persons happy is good. Perhaps if we believe that strongly enough and say so often enough, not in lectures and sermons but through the medium of interesting and readable stories, other people will come to believe it, too.[81]

This is true of all Taylor's novels. She provides representation and resources, and in doing so, she resists the classic pulp narrative, draws a clear picture of gay life in Chicago, and opens a path for further activism.

80   Forrest, *Lesbian Pulp Fiction*, xviii.
81   Taylor, 'Five minority groups', 22.

6. Saving Gay's the Word: the campaign to protect a bookshop and the right to import queer literature[1]

Graham McKerrow

Her Majesty's Customs and Excise was a British government department from 1909 until 2005, when it merged with the Inland Revenue to form HM Revenue and Customs.[2] In April 1984, officers from Customs and Excise raided Gay's the Word, a small independent bookshop in Marchmont Street, Bloomsbury, as well as the homes of two of its directors, and seized thousands of imported books in a move they called Operation Tiger. They subsequently also seized more imported LGBT+ books destined for Gay's the Word and other booksellers, one of which was put out of business. Only Gay's the Word challenged the seizures in court to stop the books being destroyed and to defend the right to import LGBT+ books. Customs and Excise then brought 100 charges against nine staff and unpaid directors of the shop in a move that presaged a major censorship trial at the Central Criminal Court.

This happened during a period of right-wing government following Margaret Thatcher's election victory in 1979 and heightened homophobia from queerbashers in the street, the media, political and religious leaders and the authorities. However, the shop had launched a defence campaign and fund following Operation Tiger and won support from the community, the publishing industry, civil libertarians, politicians and others, and after two and a half years all charges were dropped and the books returned, most of them to the shop, some to the American supplier. This is a story of attempted censorship, a determined and sustained political response and a victory for free speech and an oppressed community.

1   I thank Jim MacSweeney, Gay's the Word's manager for the last 30 years, for information and advice in preparing this account and the presentation that preceded it, and for access to Gay's the Word's archive. I am also grateful to Charles Brown and Gerard Walsh for information and original source material from their archive, Amanda Russell, Lesley Jones and Peter Dorey for advice and information, and Andrew Lumsden, a trustee of the defence fund, for advice and encouragement. Thanks also to Leila Kassir and Richard Espley of Senate House Library for enabling me to record these events, and for their patience and guidance, and to my partner Marc Ennals for his patience and advice.
2   The Commissioners for Revenue and Customs Act 2005, London. See <http://www.legislation.gov.uk/ukpga/2005/11/contents> (accessed 9 Apr. 2020).

A new shop, a new government, a new decade

In 1979, Ernest Hole and a small group of friends opened Gay's the Word bookshop to sell gay and feminist literature at 66 Marchmont Street, London WC1, premises it still occupies today. It took its name from the Ivor Novello musical *Gay's the Word* and grew out of a portable collection of books that Hole carried to different venues and events, funded by himself and Peter Dorey who had just received a small inheritance. At the time, LGBT+ books were not generally available in British bookshops but a few radical booksellers stocked some titles, and *Gay News*, a fortnightly newspaper founded by a collective of activists in June 1972, had an extensive mail-order list. Some gay literature was published in this country but much more was produced abroad, especially in the United States. Onlywomen Press had started publishing in the UK in 1974 and the community's publishers were to blossom in the 1980s with the founding of Gay Men's Press and Brilliance Books. The shop had a strict policy not to stock any material that was racist, sexist or pornographic. Gay's the Word not only stocked its politics on its shelves, it also provided its premises for other lesbian and gay political and community purposes: it was home to the Lesbian Discussion Group, the Gay Men's Disabled Group, the Gay Black Group, and for many years the Lesbian and Gay Pride Committee held its meetings there.[3]

Ernest Hole lived in New York for a while between 1968 and 1969 and became friends with Craig Rodwell, who had opened the Oscar Wilde Memorial Bookshop in Greenwich Village in 1967. 'His example inspired me to try and create a similar bookshop in London,' Hole told *Polari* magazine. Hole was not alone; lesbian and gay bookstores were being opened around the world with similar political and community motives and as part of a growing cultural surge of writing and publishing. Giovanni's Room bookstore, named after James Baldwin's classic gay novel, was opened in Philadelphia in 1973 by three members of Gay Activists Alliance and was bought for $500 three years later by Ed Hermance. When he purchased a building for the shop in 1979, one hundred volunteers helped to renovate it. In the 1980s, Giovanni's Room became a centre of the city's response to the Aids crisis because it offered information that local healthcare workers were forbidden to provide. One outlet for its stock and an alternative income stream was the export of books to other booksellers, including Gay's the Word. Norman Laurilla and George Leigh opened A Different Light bookstore, named after Elizabeth Lynn's gay science fiction novel, in Los Angeles in 1979, with further stores opening in New York and San Francisco. At their peak, they were running 300 author events per year at the three sites. In 1980 and 1981, Gay's the Word and Edinburgh's First of May radical bookshop supported the Lavender Books collective, which ran LGBT+ bookstalls in the city and at conferences and

3   Ernest Hole, 'The birth of Gay's the Word', *Polari* 17 Jan. 2012, online <http://www.polarimagazine.com/features/birth-gays-word> (accessed 9 Apr. 2020) and *Bookseller*, London, 22 Sept. 1984, 1331.

marches around the UK. After dissenting members resigned, Sigrid Nielsen and Bob Orr opened Lavender Menace bookshop in Edinburgh in 1982. So, one can see the earlier mail-order services developing into a network of mutually supportive booksellers, publishers, writers and activists using physical spaces to sell and buy books, to meet, to exchange information and to organise.[4]

In the same year that Gay's the Word opened on Marchmont Street, Margaret Thatcher came to power leading a radical right-wing government that would transform British politics in the 1980s. It was a difficult time for British LGBT+ people: queerbashing and murders were rife, as described in a Campaign for Homosexual Equality (CHE) report entitled *Attacks on Gay People*.[5] At the same time, the police used their powers to harass the community. Incidents included police incursions into clubs and saunas, for example Monroe's in Northampton,[6] and several raids on the Gemini in Huddersfield, which was allied with so-called 'fishing trips' for suspected homosexuals through people's private address books and a no-go area of the town.[7] Between 30 and 40 police stormed into the Albion sauna in New Brighton, Wallasey.[8] Shops were also under attack; for example, the Adelaide bookshop in Cecil Court, near Leicester Square, London, was subjected to repeated and coordinated raids that included the owner's and his neighbour's home. The owner and the shop were ordered to pay fines and costs totalling £11,500.[9] In London and Manchester, they even used *agents provocateurs* – young, handsome, male officers dressed in leather jackets and torn denim, known as 'the pretty police' – to entrap gay men and charge them with importuning for an immoral purpose.[10]

The courts were hostile. Divorcing mothers who were shown in court to be lesbian would lose custody of their children.[11] Anyone who had killed a gay man could use the 'homosexual panic' defence saying that he had made a pass at them, their exit had been blocked so they panicked and killed him. This way they could get a light sentence or be freed.[12] People were sacked for being lesbian or gay and when one, John Saunders, a handyman at a

4   Giovanni's Room records *c.* 1975–91, Ms Coll 17, John J Wilcox Jr LGBT Archives, Philadelphia; Tyler Gillespie, 'The last day at Giovanni's Room, America's oldest gay bookstore', *Rolling Stone*, New York, 21 May 2014; 'Lavender Menace returns: a short history', <https://somewhereedi.org/lavender-menace-returns> (accessed 9 Apr. 2020); Sam Whiting, 'A Different Light bookstore in Castro closing', 22 Apr. 2011, <https://www.sfgate.com/news/article/A-Different-Light-gay-bookstore-in-Castro-closing-2374151.php> (accessed 9 Apr. 2020).

5   *Gay News*, 198: 1, 9.

6   *Gay News*, 199: 5.

7   *Gay News*, 209: 1.

8   *Capital Gay*, 28 Jan. 1983, 1.

9   *Capital Gay*, 4 Sept. 1981, 1.

10 *Capital Gay*, 27 Jan. 1984, 1.

11 *Gay News*, 193: 5.

12 *Gay News*, 197: 14.

school camp in Aberfoyle, was dismissed in the same year that Gay's the Word opened its door, he took his case to court. In May 1981 the Court of Session in Scotland ruled, in a judgment that set a precedent for the whole country, that it was reasonable to assume homosexuals were automatically a risk to children so it was fair to sack him without needing proof of a complaint about his behaviour.[13]

The political movement responded in many ways to such provocations. The three leading membership organisations, CHE, the Scottish Homosexual Rights Group and the Northern Ireland Gay Rights Association worked together to lobby parliament and government, demanding an end to laws that discriminated against homosexuals, the introduction of employment protection, and protection from all forms of discrimination against homosexuals.[14] Lobbying achieved the decriminalisation of male homosexuality in Scotland in 1980 – this had been achieved in England and Wales in 1967.[15] The Greater London Council (GLC) introduced employment protection for its staff[16] and gave £450,000 towards a London Lesbian and Gay Centre.[17] The activist Jeff Dudgeon defeated the British government at the European Court of Human Rights, which ruled that Ulster's laws against gay male sex broke Privacy Clause 8 of the European human rights code.[18]

In March 1984, 50 police raided Movements disco at The Bell pub in King's Cross, London, which was popular with lesbian and gay activists. They were shocked at the scale and nature of the raid,[19] although it was no different from the pattern of other police incursions around the country. The following month, there was to be a new development in the State's harassment of the community: coordinated raids by Customs and Excise on a small community bookshop and the homes of some of its directors who were unpaid volunteers.[20]

Operation Tiger – absurd but serious[21]

At 9.20am on Tuesday 10 April 1984, Customs and Excise launched what they called Operation Tiger, when two Customs officers called at the home of Glenn McKee, a director of Gay's the Word, who had a flat in the Brunswick Centre a few hundred yards down Marchmont Street from the bookshop. They demanded entry and then kept McKee in his home for six hours while they searched the premises. He said, 'They went through everything – every

13   *Gay News*, 215: 3.
14   *Gay News*, 193: 3.
15   *Gay News*, 202: 3.
16   *Capital Gay*, 18 Sept. 1981, 1.
17   *Capital Gay*, 4 March 1983, 1.
18   *Capital Gay*, 23 Oct. 1981, 1.
19   *Capital Gay*, 16 March 1984, 1.
20   *Capital Gay*, 13 Apr. 1984, 1.
21   *Capital Gay*, 13 Apr. 1984, 1 and 'Defend Gay's the Word Briefing Note 1' rev. May 1985.

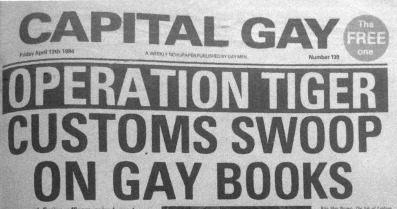

Figure 6.1. Hold the front page: Capital Gay's *report of the raids, 13 April 1984.*

piece of paper, my videos, minutes of board meetings. And they wouldn't let me talk to anyone.' Another team of Customs agents went to the bookshop. 'It was about one o'clock lunchtime that they got here,' said shop manager Paud Hegarty. 'They "advised" me to close up and the customers to leave – there were about ten customers in here.'

Customs and Excise only had jurisdiction over imported titles, not those published in this country, so they first sorted through all the books to separate out the imported ones. They then divided these into two sub-groups: those to be left at Gay's the Word and those to be detained by Customs. Dave Odd, a dark-suited agent, appeared to be in charge of the raid. The literary shortlisting was supervised by a balding man with unkempt sideburns, dirty sneakers and an oddly patterned shirt, who spent much of his time on all fours on the carpet browsing through a few paragraphs in each book. 'They clearly didn't know what they were doing,' said Hegarty 'They had to keep ringing up to find out what they were meant to take.'

The *Capital Gay* report describes what some of the agents were wearing because of the contrast with the uniformed police who usually raided gay premises, and the uniformed Customs officers that people were accustomed to seeing at ports. They took away the impounded books in a beige Vauxhall car, and placed a polythene bag containing the company records on the floor in front of the passenger seat. Till rolls, invoices, address books, the subscription list to the Gay's the Word newsletter, VAT records and correspondence with overseas gay organisations were all included. The detained books included the feminist novel *Southern Discomfort* by Rita Mae Brown, the sex guide *The Joy of Lesbian Sex* by Dr Emily Sisley and Bertha Harris, Armistead Maupin's classic novel *Tales of the City*, Gordon Meyrick's popular novel *One for the Gods*, the humorous *Cruise to Win* by Larry Giteck, Paul Monette's racy adventure story *Taking Care of Mrs Carroll*, the romantic novel *Return to Lesbos* by Valerie Taylor, and Sandra Scoppettone's coming out novel *Happy Endings Are All Alike*. They would be further evaluated to decide whether they should be 'seized' and subsequently destroyed or returned to the shop.[22]

Amanda Russell, another manager of the shop, spent most of that afternoon at Customs and Excise headquarters in nearby Woburn Place where she was questioned by Operation Tiger officers. Later, her flat was searched and several video recordings of the American soap opera *Dallas* were seized. Operation Tiger agents also visited Gay's the Word director, Dr Jonathan Cutbill, at his home in Blackheath, south London. He was a book collector and the agents were soon on the phone to their headquarters saying that they would have trouble finding pornography among the ten thousand books they estimated he had in his house. By this time, they were tired and did not remove any of his property.

22 *Capital Gay*, 8 June 1984, 1.

The fightback starts immediately

The directors shelved plans to expand the shop into new, larger premises so they could focus on defending Gay's the Word and the right to import LGBT+ books. There were protests at home and abroad, although the mainstream domestic press 'maintain[ed] a blanket silence' on the events, according to *Capital Gay*. Five days after the raids, more than 150 people attended a public meeting at County Hall, home of the GLC, then run by a controversially lesbian-and-gay-friendly Labour administration. They heard first-hand accounts of the raids and set up action committees to support the shop.[23]

A Defend Gay's the Word (DGTW) fighting fund raised £500 within the first week, and the Scala cinema at King's Cross, London, promised the proceeds from a performance. This was to become the campaign that would focus attention on Operation Tiger for the next two years. Delegates to the annual general meeting of the National Council for Civil Liberties (NCCL, now called Liberty) on the Sunday following the raid expressed their 'alarm at this evidence of increasing censorship' and called for a review of Customs and Excise's powers of search and seizure. Larry Gostin, NCCL general secretary, wrote to the chancellor of the exchequer, who was responsible for Customs and Excise, and to the home secretary, saying the raid on the shop was 'a blow to freedom of expression and to the vital work it does of improving accessibility of serious literature of interest to lesbian and gay people. It is an unabashed attempt to financially ruin one of the great educational and social institutions' of the gay community. The Campaign for Homosexual Equality wanted the matter raised in the House of Commons and asked Frank Dobson, the Labour MP for Holborn and St Pancras and thus the shop's local MP, to table a question for the chancellor, Nigel Lawson.[24]

It was now clear that the detained books represented about a third of the shop's stock, and according to *Capital Gay* the shop's tight financial position was a concern because the raids had followed a flood which had destroyed stock at the beginning of the month. Furthermore, about £11,000 worth of stock at wholesale prices had been seized on its way to the shop.[25]

More than one hundred people demonstrated outside Customs and Excise's offices in Woburn Place at lunchtime on 27 April 1984. A trade union shop steward at Customs, who refused to give her name, claimed incorrectly that the case was *sub judice* and refused to meet a delegation, either from the DGTW campaign or from the Civil Service Gay Group. The campaign was starting to attract some media attention with reports in *City Limits* magazine and the *New Statesman* and a long letter published in the *Guardian*. Three and a half weeks after the raids, the defence fund stood at more than £800 and another public meeting was called at County Hall for 20 May.[26]

23 *Capital Gay*, 20 Apr. 1984, 1.
24 Ibid.
25 *Bookseller*, 22 Sept. 1984, 1330.
26 *Capital Gay*, 4 May 1984, 1.

In early June, Customs told the bookshop that it was officially seizing 22 of the titles, according to *Capital Gay*, or 21 according to DGTW briefing note 3, amounting to 221 of the volumes detained in the raids. It said they were indecent and would therefore be destroyed unless the shop went to court to challenge the decision. The threatened titles included *One for the Gods*, *The Joy of Lesbian Sex* and a foreign edition of Carter Wilson's historical novel *Treasures on Earth*, which had also already been published in the UK.[27]

Customs issued a circular to people protesting against the raids, saying they had found a single consignment of books imported from the US by Gay's the Word and had followed this discovery by making inquiries at the shop. 'It was decided to remove the books and records for examination elsewhere in order to minimise the disturbance. This has been completed and most of the books and records have been returned to the shop.' Supporters of the shop contradicted these claims. They stated that most of the records and half the books by value had not been returned; and the fact that Customs had private bookshop correspondence dating back three years suggested that Customs' activities were not a recent event triggered by opening a single parcel of books.[28]

The parliamentary campaign was also gaining support. Three Liberal MPs, Alex Carlile (Montgomery), the Liberal home affairs spokesman, Simon Hughes (Bermondsey) and Michael Meadowcroft (Leeds West), the assistant Liberal whip, tabled a series of parliamentary questions to the chancellor of the exchequer and the home secretary. They were also seeking all-party support for an early day motion deploring the raid and calling for the return of the seized books, and they organised a meeting at the House of Commons to explain the raids and their implications to other MPs.[29]

Another action by Customs and Excise was hardly noticed at the time and reported by *Capital Gay* as only a footnote at the bottom of a longer news report about Gay's the Word, but it seems more significant in light of subsequent confiscations by Customs officers: on Monday 4 June 1984, Customs detained 120 lesbian and feminist titles in transit from Giovanni's Room, the lesbian and gay bookshop in Philadelphia that also supplied Gay's the Word and Lavender Menace, to the London International Feminist Book Fair. All these books were, however, released the following day.[30]

The fire spreads

Seizures of LGBT+ books by Customs and Excise were nothing new. For example, some of the books imported by *Gay News* for their mail-order customers were seized and destroyed by Customs in the 1970s. *Gay News*

---

27 *Capital Gay*, 8 June 1984, 1; 'DGTW Briefing Note 3, Seized Titles', rev. May 1985.
28 *Capital Gay*, 8 June 1984, 1.
29 *Capital Gay*, 15 June 1984, 1.
30 *Capital Gay*, 8 June 1984, 1.

could not trace any pattern in terms of what material was seized and what was permitted, so for some time they refrained from taking the matter to court, deciding to accept the losses as part of the price of running a mail-order book service. However, they did on one occasion challenge a seizure in the magistrates' court and chose as their battleground what they thought was an innocuous novel called *All's Well That Ends Well*. I haven't found any details about it other than it being at the time on sale at a leading London department store. *Gay News* lost the case but could see no more logic in the court's judgment than they could in the decisions of Customs and Excise. Furthermore, the costs of the action were disproportionate to the value of the books, so they refrained from contesting other seizures.[31]

Gay's the Word swiftly decided that they would stand their ground by challenging all the seizures in court – 22 titles comprising more than 200 volumes. They estimated this would cost up to £5,000, of which the defence fund had raised £2,000. They made clear that 'we have decided to go ahead with this on a political principle even though it is going to be quite serious for the shop financially.' However, Customs and Excise escalated the conflict. The mail-order bookseller Essentially Gay, run by the gay activist and writer Terry Sanderson, announced in the week beginning 18 June 1984 that it would have to close after Customs agents seized £1,600 worth of books imported from Giovanni's Room in Philadelphia and Bookpeople in California. Sanderson said he would not go to court because he did not believe a fair trial was possible. Titles included the guides *Men Loving Men* by Mitch Walker and *The Joy of Gay Sex* by Dr Charles Silverstein and Edmund White.[32]

The following month, Customs surveyors seized a consignment of books sent from Giovanni's Room to Balham Food and Books Cooperative, an alternative bookshop in south London. Balham Food and Books said they could not afford to challenge the seizure in court.[33] Housmans bookshop at King's Cross, London, announced at the end of July that Customs surveyors had also impounded some of its books, and that the costs of challenging the seizures in court were prohibitive. On 1 August, Customs notified Gay's the Word that it was seizing 15 copies of Issue 123 of the French gay newspaper *Gai Pied*. These were intercepted at the port of Dover in June. This spread the seizures from books to newspapers. In a statement, Gay's the Word said this represented an expansion of the censorship from matters relating to sex and alleged indecency to straightforward political issues.[34]

In September, it was reported that Customs surveyors at Prestwick airport in Scotland had seized £250 worth of books and magazines on their way to Lavender Menace bookshop in Edinburgh. The titles affected included copies

31 Written statement by Charles Brown to the committal hearing, June 1985, 7 and oral statement by Michael Mason, news editor in the 1970s, to Charles Brown on 18 June 1995, and recorded in an undated witness statement.
32 *Capital Gay*, 22 June 1984, 1.
33 *Capital Gay*, 20 July 1984, 3.
34 *Capital Gay*, 3 Aug. 1984, 1.

of the magazine *Sinister Wisdom*, one of the oldest and best-known lesbian magazines, edited at one time by Adrienne Rich. One of the shop's co-owners, Sigrid Nielsen, commented to *Capital Gay*: 'I was stunned when I heard the news; no lesbian publications have ever been seized from Lavender Menace bookshop before. And certainly nothing of this high quality.'[35]

Since April, there had been seven seizures and detentions of lesbian and gay literature by Customs and Excise surveyors but in September 1984, Mr J.S. England, the chief press officer for Customs, told *Capital Gay*: 'There is no campaign against any particular group.'[36] The following month, Customs seized 132 titles, amounting to 2,265 items, from Gay's the Word. *Capital Gay* reported that this would take the legal costs of challenging the seizures in court up from the previous estimate of £5,000 to about £30,000. The newspaper said this threw the shop 'into turmoil', but Jonathan Cutbill was quoted as asking, 'Can we afford *not* to fight?' *Capital Gay* said these latest seizures were so wide-ranging that they were likely to fuel support for the bookshop because they included works by writers such as Robin Maugham, James Kirkwood, Jean-Paul Sartre and Gore Vidal, and books on health, guides for parents, cartoon books and newspapers.[37]

In November 1984, Customs surveyors seized 15 copies of *The Joy of Gay Sex* which were on their way to the Gay Christian Movement (GCM). This was the first time a national gay membership organisation had been subjected to Customs and Excise seizures. Rev. Richard Kirker, GCM secretary, told a DGTW meeting that Customs offered not to prosecute him if he gave evidence against Gay's the Word. 'In other words, it was blackmail and I have no intention of giving into that,' he said. He committed GCM to contesting the seizure, working closely with DGTW and mobilising GCM members to support the campaign. Customs also seized a further five titles, 19 volumes, being imported by Lavender Menace in Edinburgh (its precursor was Lavender Books, the shop Gay's the Word had supported). This brought the total number of detentions and seizures of LGBT+ consignments since April to ten.[38] Some of the seizure notices covered separate consignments of the same titles, and when this was taken into account, Customs surveyors had seized 142 – although some reports say 144 – titles from Gay's the Word in three actions between April and October 1984.

Criminal conspiracy charges

On Wednesday 21 November 1984, Paud Hegarty, the manager of Gay's the Word, and its eight directors were charged with conspiracy to import indecent and obscene material. The directors were Charles Brown, Jonathan Cutbill,

35 *Capital Gay*, 14 Sept. 1984, 3.
36 *Capital Gay*, 21 Sept. 1984, 5.
37 'DGTW Briefing Note 3' rev. May 1985, and *Capital Gay*, 12 Oct. 1984, 1.
38 *Capital Gay*, 9 Nov. 1984, 1.

Peter Dorey, Gerard Walsh, Glenn McKee, Amanda Russell, John Duncan and Lesley Jones. Amanda Russell had found new employment so she and the latter two were now former managers of the bookshop.

The defendants all faced identical charges of conspiring to import indecent or obscene material, with six of them facing a further eight, and three of them nine charges of importing named titles that Customs claimed were indecent or obscene. The total of 84 charges would in time grow to be 100 charges against the nine defendants. The scale of Customs and Excise's legal action set the scene for a major trial at the Old Bailey, which the *Guardian*, as reported in *Capital Gay*, compared to the infamous 1960 obscenity trial against Penguin Books for publication of D.H. Lawrence's *Lady Chatterley's Lover*.[39]

Each defendant was charged that:

> On divers dates between 1 January 1981 and 1 August 1984 at London and elsewhere [they did] conspire with [each other] and with Ed Hermance [of Giovanni's Room in Philadelphia] and other persons unknown fraudulently to evade the prohibition on importation of indecent and obscene material imposed by section 42 of the Customs Consolidation Act 1876, that being an offence contrary to section 170 (2) of the Customs and Excise Management Act 1979.

The maximum penalty for each of the charges involving individual titles was two years in prison, a £1,000 fine or a fine of three times the value of the books. The maximum penalty for conspiracy was life imprisonment. The estimated legal costs rose to between £30,000 and £50,000.[40]

I knew some of the nine defendants before Operation Tiger. Others I met as the case progressed. Here, I want to record a little about them individually and as a group; the sources of this information are the individuals concerned and my own observations. I was not a party to their meetings among themselves or with their lawyers, but while at *Gay News* and then *Capital Gay* I interviewed several of them and met others, and when I became one of the campaign coordinators I liaised with them, and on occasion we socialised together. Some became good friends.

Some of the defendants had collaborated before Gay's the Word was started. Charles Brown, Jonathan Cutbill, Peter Dorey, John Duncan and Paud Hegarty had, like Ernest Hole, been members of Gay Icebreakers, the radical lesbian and gay telephone helpline and befriending collective that another defendant, Glenn McKee, approached for support in the late 1970s. The title 'director' may give the impression they were business people but they were unpaid volunteers who guided the shop and worked in it by rota on Sundays. Some of them had painted the premises and built the bookshelves that exist to this day. A looming high-profile case at the Old Bailey and the possibility of severe penalties must have put a great deal of stress on each

39 *Capital Gay*, 30 Nov. 1984, 3.
40 *Capital Gay,* 30 Nov. 1984, 3.

of the defendants but I never heard any of them express any self-pity or fear, although they voiced anger as Customs increased the pressure with their astonishing array of seizures and charges. All nine displayed dignity and determination throughout their ordeal.

Charles Brown, originally from Lanarkshire, was an economist for British Rail and later a senior civil servant; he maintained a warm, friendly sense of humour throughout; he lived then and still lives with his partner Gerard Walsh.

Jonathan Cutbill had been involved with Gay's the Word from its early days, was an information systems expert at Greenwich's National Maritime Museum, and was an authority on the poet Wilfred Owen. He amassed an unrivalled collection of rare and interesting books on LGBT+ subjects which, upon his death aged 82 in August 2019, numbered about 30,000. These went to the University of London's Senate House Library.

Peter Dorey funded Gay's the Word when it was a portable bookseller visiting gay venues and conferences before it found permanent premises. He was a sound technician for the BBC and was perhaps the quietest in a group of strong characters. Peter provided invaluable advice and information for the preparation of this account but before it was published he died in his sleep on the night of 11/12 February 2021 after being ill for several years.

John Duncan was manager of the shop when it recovered from some early commercial stumbles and later went on to be circulation manager of the *New Statesman*. He had a great sense of humour and fun. He would have been a central figure in the trial because he wrote letters to Ed Hermance of Giovanni's Room asking for help in avoiding detection by Customs using the ploy of sending 'ordinary books' to Glenn's flat but 'For all "obscene books" (e.g. JGS, Meat, most Gay Sunshine material, or anything else that could possibly be labelled pornographic) please send to J. Runcie, [delivery address, Duncan's home in London N1].' Runcie was the name of the then archbishop of Canterbury. John died aged 32 of Aids-related complications on 18 January 1993.

Paud Hegarty was also a manager of the shop, who after the case was compounded trained as a lawyer but died from Aids-related complications in 2000 aged 45. He was a tall, gentle man originally from the Republic of Ireland with a dry wit and a fine understanding of Marxist theory.

Lesley Jones was the subscriptions manager at *Gay News* when I met her in 1980. She and Amanda Russell were lovers and it was through Russell that Jones volunteered at Gay's the Word, where she later became a director. She always had a smile and a kind word. Some years later she emigrated with a new partner to Canada but now lives and works in Leeds.

Figure 6.2. A campaign publicity shot of the defendants holding some of the seized titles: centre: Amanda Russell; clockwise from top with goatee beard: Jonathan Cutbill, Charles Brown, John Duncan, Lesley Jones, Paud Hegarty, Peter Dorey, Glenn McKee and Gerard Walsh.

Glenn McKee was originally from Downpatrick in Northern Ireland and when he came to London he approached Gay Icebreakers. This led to him getting involved in the bookshop where he started the Gay Men's Disabled Group, which was the first of its kind.

Amanda Russell was one of the funniest, friendliest, toughest lesbians one could hope to meet who, after managing the shop, went to work for Lesbian Line and then moved to Hebden Bridge, West Yorkshire. She and Jones started the Lesbian Discussion Group that still meets at the shop on Wednesday evenings, which makes it the oldest such group in existence.

Gerard Walsh, a native Londoner, was an economist and writer for the Economist Intelligence Unit, who lives now as he did then with his partner Charles Brown.

Figure 6.3. Capital Gay *published Customs' secret guidelines to its staff telling them what material to confiscate.*

The case goes to court

In March the following year, Customs surveyors at the port of Dover seized a second shipment of the French weekly newspaper *Gai Pied* on its way to Gay's the Word, saying that Issue 157 was indecent or obscene.[41]

The *Bookseller* magazine had led the way in the mainstream book publishing world with coverage of Operation Tiger across three pages in November 1984, beginning with: 'The Customs raid on Gay's the Word shop in London, and temporary seizure of much of the stock, will not

ry, 29 March 1985, 1.

attract the sympathy of everyone. However, an important principle may be involved.'[42] In the spring of the following year, mainstream publishers came to the defence of Gay's the Word: Penguin Books gave £500 to the defence fund, Gollancz gave £500, Chatto and Windus gave £200, and Faber promised to donate as well. The book publishing world was rallying to the bookshop's cause. The fund had now surpassed £30,000.[43]

In June, *Capital Gay* published secret guidelines given by Customs and Excise to their surveyors to help them decide what material should be detained or seized as 'indecent or obscene'. Members of Parliament had asked for these guidelines to be provided by the government but Barney Hayhoe, the treasury minister responsible for Customs, had refused to supply them to the MPs. The guidelines were leaked to *Capital Gay*, which I edited, and we published them. The relevant section of the document was Section 1, 2. (b), which listed what Customs regarded as indecent or obscene opening with: 'Books and magazines. Sexual activities, including variations e.g. masturbation, lesbianism, homosexuality...' before going on to list a variety of 'deviations' such as bondage, whipping, beating and domination.[44]

The following week, the committal hearing opened at North London magistrates' court in Stoke Newington with NCCL handling the defence under their lawyers Marie Staunton and Hilary Kitchen. The defendants had opted for an old-style committal hearing, which meant that the prosecution had to present its entire case with witnesses who could be cross-examined by the defence. Geoffrey Robertson was the barrister for Gay's the Word. He had previously represented *Oz* magazine at the famous obscenity trial in 1971, and *Gay News* when it was prosecuted for blasphemous libel in 1977. Under his cross-examination, Customs surveyors admitted that gay books entering the country were automatically detained and sent to Customs head office.[45]

One exchange between Robertson and a Customs surveyor called Aftar Singh Huntal went:

> GR: Why is it necessary to send books to head office?
> ASH: Gay books we send to head office.
> GR: You mean addressed to Gay's the Word?
> ASH: Any company, not necessarily Gay's the Word.
> GR: Is it customary to stop gay books and send them to headquarters?
> ASH: Yes.[46]

Stuart Lawson Rogers, prosecuting, alleged that the defendants had conspired to use 'safe addresses' and aliases to import indecent or obscene material.

42 *Bookseller*, 22 Sept. 1984, 1330.
43 *Capital Gay*, 24 May 1985, 1.
44 *Capital Gay*, 21 June 1985, 17.
45 *Capital Gay*, 28 June 1985, 1.
46 *Capital Gay*, 28 June 1985, 1.

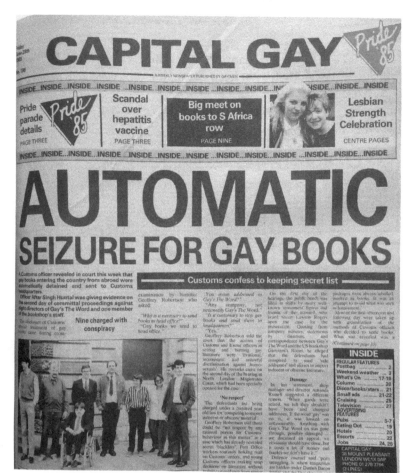

Figure 6.4. A Customs officer admitted at the committal hearing that all gay books were seized.

One of the defendants, Amanda Russell, gave a different explanation for their behaviour. She said:

> When goods were seized, we felt they shouldn't have been and changed addresses. If the word 'gay' was on it, it was looked on unfavourably. Anything with 'Gay's the Word' on was gone through, possibly damaged … we discussed an appeal, we obviously should have done, but it costs a lot of money and frankly we don't have it.[47]

Defence counsel said: 'Porn smuggling is when magazines are hidden under Danish bacon lorries and the like. They are not labelled. Gay's the Word packages were always labelled, marked as books. It was an attempt to avoid

[7] *Capital Gay*, 28 June 1985, 1.

what was seen as harassment.'[48]

So the legal arguments were clear. There was little disagreement over the facts of what the defendants had done; the dispute was over their motives. The prosecution said they were trying to import indecent or obscene material without being detected; the defence said they were trying to import books and took steps to avoid official harassment targeting lesbian and gay books.

On 3 July, the officer in charge of Operation Tiger took the witness stand. Geoffrey Robertson, for the defence, produced a copy of the previous Friday's *Capital Gay*, which reproduced the Customs guidelines on what surveyors should detain. Colin Woodgate, a higher executive Customs officer, refused to confirm that they were the authentic Customs guidelines but, when pressed by the defence barrister, he admitted that they 'seem[ed] to be' the guidelines. *Capital Gay* was shown to the magistrate and became an official exhibit. Woodgate confirmed that all officers were given photocopied guidelines telling them to look out for 'masturbation, homosexuality, lesbianism and group sex'.[49]

It emerged that Operation Tiger had been organised at quite a low administrative level, and many of the surveyors who issued seizure notices 'turned out to be young men of 20 who left school at 16', according to Barry Scanes, treasurer of the defence campaign. 'These, it transpired, were the people who decided that poems by Verlaine were "indecent" and had gone through Genet's *Querelle de Brest* marking what they considered to be the rude bits.'[50] Officers giving evidence said they were given no training or guidance as to legal definitions of indecency, obscenity or literary merit.[51]

On 20 August 1985 the magistrate, Mr C.J. Bourke, committed the nine defendants for trial at the Central Criminal Court, popularly known as the Old Bailey. He said that the issues were whether or not the publications were indecent, whether or not the defendants would have anticipated that the generality of public opinion would have considered them obscene, and finally he said the judgment should be made according to the views of heterosexuals:

> A committed homosexual may consider that detailed accounts of homosexual behaviour in such a way as to arouse homosexual feeling was [sic] proper. He would dispute the classification as indecent or obscene and challenge their description as such. That is not the point. The question is not what *he* thought, but what others, not of his prediliction [sic] would think.[52]

In a statement to the court on behalf of all the defendants, McKee said: 'We are booksellers, not pornographers.'

48   *Capital Gay*, 28 June 1985, 1.
49   'GTW defendants kept waiting', *Capital Gay*, 5 July 1985.
50   Letter from Barry Scanes to Gay's the Word supporters, 1 Aug. 1985.
51   'Customs officers in the dark on indecency', *Guardian*, 25 June 1985.
52   Note of Committal, Mr C. Bourke, 20 Aug. 1985.

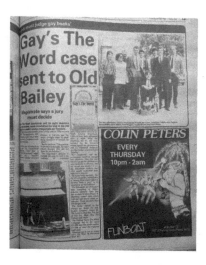

Figure 6.5. The magistrate sent the nine booksellers for trial at the Old Bailey.

The political campaign

The directors and staff of Gay's the Word kept the shop open throughout this time while also preparing their legal defence and guiding the political defence campaign. They travelled the country speaking to lesbian and gay groups and others about the case. The DGTW campaign and the defence fund were organised as separate elements, with independent trustees appointed to supervise the fund.

The campaign encouraged letter writing, lobbying, media coverage and occasional street protests, such as those outside Customs headquarters following the Operation Tiger raids, and supporters gathering at the magistrates court for the committal hearing. However, its main thrust was the parliamentary campaign, which aimed to bring political influence to bear on the treasury and, through the treasury, on Customs and Excise itself, as well as to highlight the iniquities of the Customs Consolidation Act 1876 in the hope of achieving reforms to the law.

Defend Gay's the Word had six aims:[53]

1. The return of Gay's the Word's books and records and the personal possessions of its directors and staff; the release of any material detained at point of entry; no further detention of imports to Gay's the Word or other importers.
2. All the charges to be dropped.
3. Compensation for lost revenues due to the action.
4. To increase public awareness of the action and of HM Customs and Excise powers generally, and to mobilise opposition to both within the gay and lesbian as well as non-gay communities.
5. To put the action against Gay's the Word firmly in the context of overall police and government actions against the civil liberties of lesbians and gay men.
6. To lobby for the laws governing HM Customs and Excise to be brought into line with accepted principles of civil liberties and natural justice.

As already stated, the parliamentary campaign started directly after the Operation Tiger raids in April 1984. Within days, CHE had asked Frank Dobson, the bookshop's constituency MP, to table a question in the House to the chancellor of the exchequer, Nigel Lawson. Larry Gostin, NCCL general secretary, wrote to the home secretary and the chancellor condemning Operation Tiger.[54] In June 1984, three Liberal MPs, Alex Carlile, Simon Hughes and Michael Meadowcroft, asked the chancellor and home secretary a series of parliamentary questions about the case. They also sought all-party support for an early day motion condemning Operation Tiger, and they arranged a meeting at the House of Commons during Lesbian and Gay Pride Week to tell other MPs about the raids. This parliamentary activity followed a recent debate in the Commons about the use of so-called 'pretty police' *agents provocateurs* used to entrap gay men, and coincided with CHE lobbying the House of Lords to amend the Police and Criminal Evidence Bill.[55]

On 12 July, Gay's the Word was the first subject discussed during Treasury Questions in the House of Commons. In response to questions from Chris Smith (Labour, Islington South and Finsbury) and Simon Hughes, Ian Stewart, the treasury's economic secretary, said that the government had received 80 letters of protest about the raids including 26 forwarded by MPs, and nine written questions. Dobson said: 'The bookshop is in my constituency. Will the minister confirm that none of my constituents has complained about it but that many parents in the area are worried about the massive increase in heroin addiction?

53 'Defend Gay's the Word Briefing Note 8 revised May 1985'.
54 *Capital Gay*, 20 Apr. 1984, 1.
55 *Capital Gay*, 15 June 1984, 1.

Does he think that Customs and Excise should give priority to stopping the import of heroin rather than playing the fool with a bookshop?'[56]

The NCCL stepped up its support for the shop in August 1984, offering the services of its lawyers and making Gay's the Word one of its two major campaigns – the other being to reinstate trade unions at the government's communications headquarters.[57]

In November, the Conservative MP John Wheeler JP (Westminster North) tabled four written questions about the seizures, but Barney Hayhoe gave what *Capital Gay* called 'evasive answers'. Christine Mackie MEP (Labour, Birmingham East) visited Gay's the Word and promised to raise the matter in the European Parliament.[58] On 13 November, an all-party group of MPs meeting at the House of Commons offered its full support to the defence campaign. They decided to table questions to the attorney general and the treasury, and to ask Nigel Lawson to receive an all-party delegation.[59] The GLC's Police Committee published on 12 March a report critical of Customs' 'harassment and censorship' of lesbian and gay bookshops and called for a government inquiry into the role of Customs and Excise.[60]

In June 1985, the shadow home secretary, Gerald Kaufman, issued a statement to coincide with the committal hearing:

> I would like to express my strong support for Gay's the Word bookshop in the difficulties in which it is involved. Enormous amounts of public money have been spent in order to interfere with the right of British citizens to read what they choose, in many cases books which are freely and uncontroversially available elsewhere. At a time of a massive crime wave in London, with an unfortunate lack of success by the police in coping with that crime wave, the authorities should direct their attention to muggers and burglars rather than authors and booksellers.[61]

Frank Dobson and Chris Smith spoke at a press conference organised by the defence campaign that same week. According to *Capital Gay*, Smith said he could not understand Customs' priorities. Over the previous five years the department had shed 1,000 jobs. With alarm growing over international drug trafficking, the government was now trumpeting that it had employed a mere 160 new officers. And yet at least 37 officers had been involved in the Gay's the Word action.[62]

As already demonstrated, the shop and the defence campaign received support from the book publishing industry. There were also letters of support

56 *Capital Gay*, 20 July 1984, 3.
57 *Capital Gay*, 10 Aug. 1984, 1.
58 *Capital Gay*, 9 Nov. 1984, 1.
'   *Capital Gay*, 16 Nov. 1984, 1.
    Capital Gay, 29 March 1985, p. 1.
       statement from Gerald Kaufman', 21 June 1985.
          ital Gay, 28 June 1985, 10.

and donations from writers such as Angela Carter and Gore Vidal,[63] and Sir Angus Wilson, president of the Royal Society of Literature, issued this statement to coincide with the committal hearing:

> As a writer, I have had to protest sadly often against the persecution of writers in many parts of the world. It is utterly disgraceful that in this civilised country we should have to protest against censorship of reading material. It is shameful that prosecutions can still be brought by individuals or officials under long-outdated laws. It is intolerable that officials should have such wide-ranging powers of indiscriminate seizure of books. It is even more intolerable that those powers should be exercised.[64]

The Central Criminal Court announced that the defendants would face trial starting in October 1986. In January 1986, David Northmore, an activist with Kent gay groups and the NCCL, was appointed as coordinator of the defence campaign, a full-time job and the first paid staff post.[65] The following month, I left my position as co-editor of *Capital Gay* to join the defence campaign as joint coordinator.[66] The campaign involved countless numbers of people around the world writing letters of protest, organising benefits and sending personal donations. Also taking part were volunteers at the campaign office in the shop's basement, allies in the media and politics, contributors to a one-hour BBC documentary, and even a London theatre director who was writing and recruiting cast and orchestra for *Operation Tiger – The Musical*, which was scheduled to start at the Piccadilly Theatre just before the trial.

The law takes a strange turn

There was no pause in Customs' policy of seizures while both sides prepared for the Old Bailey trial. In January 1986, five copies of *Man to Man*, a sociological research work by Dr Charles Silverstein, were intercepted at Mount Pleasant sorting office in north London en route from Giovanni's Room to Gay's the Word. Three previous consignments of this title had arrived safely at the shop, although one appeared to have been tampered with and resealed. The academic Mary McIntosh, a member of the Home Office's Policy Advisory Committee to the Criminal Law Revision Committee, told *Capital Gay*: 'I don't see why this book has been seized by Customs and Excise. Far from doing any harm it is an educational and informative book.'[67]

But then something unusual happened in another court case that was seemingly unconnected with Gay's the Word, but may have had a profound

---

63   NCCL press release, 'The literary trial of the eighties', 17 June 1985, London.
64   'A statement from Sir Angus Wilson, president of the Royal Society of Literature', 18 June 1985, London.
65   *Capital Gay*, 17 Jan. 1986, 9.
66   *Capital Gay*, 28 Feb. 1986, 1.
67   *Capital Gay*, 14 March 1986, 1.

effect on the case against the shop. A judgment involving the importation of sex dolls was appealed to the European Union in Luxembourg, which ruled that public morality was no grounds for banning the importation of goods that were otherwise allowed to be produced and sold in the country concerned. Customs surveyors at Heathrow had seized 490 West German inflatable dolls in 1983. The importer, a company called Conegate, which ran a number of sex shops in the UK, took the government to court, arguing that the Customs action broke the European Economic Community's rules on the free movement of goods. The Treaty of Rome allowed governments to ban the importation of goods in defence of public morality but the European judges ruled, on 11 March 1986, that a member state could not argue that it was prohibiting the importation of certain goods in order to defend public morality if its own legislation allowed the manufacture and marketing of such goods in its territory.[68]

Most of the titles seized from Gay's the Word had been imported from the United States but obviously it would be possible to import titles from America via another European state, so the Conegate ruling could affect imports from all countries. The judgment meant that imports would be subject to the tougher test of obscenity contained in the Obscene Publications Acts 1959 and 1964, which applies to domestically produced material. The test for indecency under the Customs Consolidation Act is defined as material likely to offend the man in the street, whereas the test for obscenity is that it must 'tend to deprave and corrupt' those likely to see it, and the obscenity acts allow publications that are 'for the public good' in the interests of science, literature, art or learning, so defendants can call expert witnesses to testify to the importance of works in these respects.[69]

A week after the judgment, the Labour MPs Chris Smith and Jo Richardson, who was a member of the party's National Executive Committee, met Peter Brooke, the newly appointed treasury minister responsible for Customs, to ask him to instruct treasury lawyers to study the Luxembourg judgment. Brooke promised that officers would stop opening every package addressed to Gay's the Word, and he also promised to reconsider the seizure of *Man to Man*.[70] However, in June, Customs officers at Gatwick broke their own rules in relation to allowing the importation of material for personal use, when they seized a copy of the American gay newspaper *The Advocate* and some soft porn magazines from an unfortunate Hackney schoolteacher returning from a holiday in the United States.[71]

The barrister Richard du Cann drafted a letter to Customs and Excise to be sent by the NCCL's legal officer, Marie Staunton, who was acting as solicitor for

---

68 'European court bars a ban on sex dolls', *Guardian*, March 1986, and 'European Law report', *The Times*, 12 March 1986.

69 *Bookseller*, 22 Sept. 1984, 1331; *Capital Gay*, 21 March 1986, 3; 'No "public good" defence to seizure of obscene imports, Law Report', *Independent*, 13 Jan. 1989.

70 *Capital Gay*, 28 March 1986, 9.

71 *Capital Gay*, 6 June 1986, 1.

the defendants. It said that in light of the Conegate judgment:

1. The case should be withdrawn against all the defendants.
2. The bookshop's costs should be paid from central funds.
3. The titles should be divided into those said to infringe the Obscenity Acts and those which do not.
4. Those said to infringe the Obscenity Acts should be returned to the sender in the United States.
5. The other titles should be released to the defendants.
6. The defendants will not reimport any of the titles in 4 above without first telling Customs.[72]

The charges are dropped, the books are returned

On 27 June, more than two years and two months after the Operation Tiger raids, the defendants and campaigners learned a new legal term when HM Customs and Excise informed lawyers for the defendants that the case would be compounded. 'Compounded' meant that all one hundred charges against all nine defendants had been dropped. Customs also said they would return all the books; 19 of the titles were to be sent back to Giovanni's Room in Philadelphia because Customs believed they were obscene under the Obscene Publications Acts, but the remainder of the 142 titles seized were to be handed over to Gay's the Word. Customs said they would apply the test of obscenity when deciding what to seize in future.[73]

The shop's window display of the released books now on sale was as happy a sight as the defendants' faces while sipping champagne with Marie Staunton and campaign workers within. And it was announced in time to add a sparkle to that year's Pride Parade on 5 July.[74] More than 2,000 people attended a Victory Ball at the Hippodrome nightclub at Leicester Square later that month, including MPs, at least one MEP and David Whitaker, editor of the Bookseller.[75]

In August, the Rev Richard Kirker, secretary of the Gay Christian Movement, went to Customs' offices in Woburn Place, London, WC1, to collect 15 copies of The Joy of Gay Sex that had been seized by surveyors.[76] New deliveries of 21 mailsacks containing about 2,000 volumes of 100 titles arrived from America at the bookshop in November, and more were anticipated. The shipments included some new titles as well as books that Customs had tried to ban from the UK, such as The Joy of Lesbian Sex, The Joy of Gay Sex and other sex manuals and studies.[77]

72 Letter from Marie Staunton to Mr Worrall, solicitor, HM Customs and Excise, 3 June 1986.
73 Capital Gay, 4 July 1986, 1.
74 Capital Gay, 4 July 1986, 1.
75 Capital Gay, 25 July 1986.
76 Capital Gay, 22 Aug. 1986, 1.
77 Capital Gay, 21 Nov. 1986, 3.

Figure 6.6. The case was compounded on the anniversary of the Stonewall riots and so in time to be celebrated on the day of the Pride Parade 1986.

In the years that followed, Gay's the Word was involved in a series of court cases aimed at clarifying the law. These started with the importation from the Netherlands in October 1986 of the books *Men in Erotic Art* (about which I have found no details), *Men Loving Men, Men Loving Themselves* by Jack Morin PhD (in which 12 gay men discuss their attitudes to masturbation), and the erotic fiction *My Brother My Self*, *Roman Conquests* and *Below the Belt*, all by Phil Andros (a pen name of Samuel Steward). Following the Conegate judgment and the compounding of the case against Gay's the Word, it was unclear if the 'public good' defence and the use of expert witnesses could be employed to defend imports. The case reached the Court of Appeal, which ruled in December 1988 that the 'public good' defence was not applicable to imports.[78]

Documentary evidence is hard to find, but a plan had been mooted, which I believe was agreed in principle with Customs and Excise, for Gay's the Word to reimport in batches the titles Customs had returned to the US, notifying Customs in advance, so that the law relating to allegedly obscene imports could be tested in court. This would have been in accord with point 6 above in the letter from Marie Staunton to the solicitor representing Customs. It seems likely that this is what led to the judgment involving these titles, but I have not found proof of this. Sources detailing what happened would be welcome.

Discussion

Operation Tiger highlighted the extraordinary powers of HM Customs and Excise, which shocked the defendants and their supporters and can be summarised as follows:

1. The Writ of Assistance is like a search warrant, except that one is issued at the start of each reign of a monarch and lasts until six months after the reign ends. It allows Customs officers to enter any building by force and search and seize any goods liable to forfeiture. This far exceeds powers granted to the police and, unlike a search warrant, is not supervised by the courts.[79]
2. Seized books are in effect 'guilty' until proven innocent; they are destroyed unless the importer takes the case to court to challenge Customs' decision.[80]
3. Until the Conegate judgment and the compounding of the case against Gay's the Word, the law treated imported goods differently from goods produced in the UK. Imported goods were banned if they were indecent, that is, if they would offend the man in the street, whereas goods produced in the UK would only be banned if they were obscene, and that was defined as tending to deprave and corrupt those likely to see it, which was harder to prove. Domestically produced goods could also be defended if they were 'for the public good' and expert witnesses could be called.[81]

It is clear from HM Customs and Excise's actions against a variety of importers that they tried to shut off the importation of all lesbian and gay books. They may not have started with that intention: as Operation Tiger unfolded,

---

78 'No "public good" defence to seizure of obscene imports, Law Report', the *Independent*, 13 Jan. 1989.

79 Customs and Excise Management Act 1979 section 161 London.

80 *Capital Gay*, 8 June 1984, 1.

81 'No "public good" defence to seizure of obscene imports, Law Report', *Independent*, 13 Jan. 1989.

Customs staff were surprised by the character of Gay's the Word and the nature of its stock – books with words. They were clearly more accustomed to dealing with photo magazines. Whereas some book importers like *Gay News* carried the loss of seizures, and some like Housmans bookshop and Balham Food and Books Cooperative could not afford to go to court, while others like Essentially Gay were driven out of business, Gay's the Word stood and fought the case. In response, Customs escalated the case with more seizures and the unprecedented array of criminal charges.

This raises the first two unanswered questions about the case: why did Customs start it and why did they escalate it? As well as looking within Customs for the answer, it is worth recalling the homophobic attitudes of the time and that the UK had a right-wing government under Margaret Thatcher – the notorious Section 28 banning local authorities from promoting homosexuality as 'a pretend family relationship' was to follow.

A third important unanswered question remains: why did Customs compound the case? In 2018, when I asked Charles Brown and Gerard Walsh why they thought the case was dropped, they immediately said 'The defence campaign'. They added that they thought DGTW's identification of and publicising of a series of absurd and humorous inconsistencies in policy embarrassed senior civil servants and ministers, which was 'a cardinal no-no in the civil service'. The suggestion is that Customs backed down to avoid further public humiliation. The change of minister at the treasury, when Peter Brooke took over responsibility for Customs and Excise from Barney Hayhoe, may also be relevant. Any new minister will be briefed on what is in their in-tray and will want to ditch anything that could prove embarrassing. The judgment of the Luxembourg court in the Conegate case may have been the reason for the compounding, or it could have been a useful excuse for a worried minister. It is notable how closely Customs' settlement followed the defence solicitor's suggestions in her letter about the implications of the Conegate judgment, except that the defendants' costs were not paid from central funds.

I have tried to find the answers to these questions but my enquiries to what is now HM Revenue and Customs were redirected to the National Archives. My online searches on the National Archives website, assisted by an enthusiastic and knowledgeable archivist providing online 'chat' assistance, failed to find anything useful. I have received no reply to my letters to Peter Brooke, who is now Baron Brooke of Sutton Mandeville. This research is far from exhaustive and I hope that others will have more success explaining why this case started, why it escalated and why it ended.

It is clear that Gay's the Word became a key part of a growing political movement and of the LGBT+ literary world, locally and internationally. It formed part of an eco-system of cooperation and exchange that enabled our emerging community to communicate and organise in new and more effective ways about an array of pertinent social and political subjects, and to provide the best information to those affected by a growing health crisis. It is also clear that the authorities' response was to mount an escalating series of actions that seemed intended to close booksellers (as happened with Essentially Gay and threatened to happen with Gay's the Word), or at the very least to intimidate them. One can imagine the effect a successful prosecution of a hundred charges against nine people at the Old Bailey would have had on Gay's the Word and other booksellers.

The titles seized by HM Customs & Excise from Gay's the Word in three separate actions between April and October 1984, as recorded in *Capital Gay*, 2 November 1984[1]

The truly unbelievable

Carpenter, Edward *Iolaus: An Anthology of Friendship*

Pizan, Christine de *The Book of the City of Ladies*

Newspapers and magazines

The Advocate

Flaunting It: A Decade of Gay Journalism from the Body Politic

Christopher Street *Aphrodisiac: Fiction from Christopher Street*

Common Lives, Lesbian Lives: A Lesbian Feminist Quarterly

Gai Pied

Gay Sunshine Journal

New York Native

History

Evans, Arthur *Witchcraft and Gay Counter Culture*

Faderman, Lillian *Surpassing the Love of Men: Romantic Friendships and Love Between Women from the Renaissance to the Present*

Faderman, Lillian *Scotch Verdict: Miss Pirie and Miss Woods v. Dame Cumming Gordon*

Rictor, Frank *The Nazi Extermination of Homosexuals*

Biography and autobiography

Brogan, Jim *Jack and Jim: A Personal Journal of the '70s*

Gay Sunshine Interviews Vol. 1 1978 & Vol. II 1982

Harrison, William *Burton & Speke*

Lane, Erskine *Game-Texts: A Guatemalan Journal*

Rorem, Ned *Paris and New York Diaries of Ned Rorem*

Rumaker, Michael *A Day and Night at the Baths*

Sartre, Jean-Paul *St Genet*

Smith, Michael J. *Black Men White Men*

Waters, John *Shock Value*

---

1   The information in this appendix comes from the original list published in *Capital Gay*, 2 Nov. 1984. The headings and title groupings are replicated as originally printed.

Notes from a Marriage
Parisian Lives

Politics and studies
Greene, Gerald & Caroline *S&M: The Last Taboo*
Morin, Jack *Men Loving Themselves*
Rivers, Julius Edwin *Proust and the Art of Love*
Tripp, C.A. *The Homosexual Matrix*
Weinberg, Thomas & Kamel, G.W. Levi *S&M: Studies in Sadomasochism*
Men Behind Bars
Men in Erotic Art
Sex Behind Bars
Women and Madness
Women Fiction
Feminism in the '80s

Humour
Christopher Street *And God Bless Uncle Harry and His Roommate Jack (Who We're Not Supposed to Talk About)*
Christopher Street *Le Gay Ghetto*
Giteck, Larry *Cruise to Win*
The Simply Divine Cut-Out Doll Book
Henly, Clark *The Butch Manual*
Tress, Arthur *Facing Up*

Books for young people
Ecker, B.A. *Independence Day*
Kirkwood, James *There Must Be a Pony*
Knudson, R.R. *You Are the Rain*
Knudson, R.R. *Fox Running*
Scoppettone, Sandra *Happy Endings are All Alike*

Health, sex and counselling guides
Blank, Joanie *The Playbook for Men About Sex*
Blank, Joanie *The Playbook for Women About Sex*
Borhek, Mary V. *Coming Out to Parents*
Cahill, Dr Kevin M. *The Aids Epidemic*

Silverstein, Dr Charles & White, Edmund *The Joy of Gay Sex*

Silverstein, Dr Charles *A Family Matter: A Parents' Guide to Homosexuality*

Sisley, Dr Emily & Harris, Bertha *The Joy of Lesbian Sex*

Walker, Mitch *Men Loving Men*

Witches Heal

Parents of the Homosexual

Sexually Transmitted Diseases

Look Me in the Eye

Poetry

Everhead, Jim *Cute*

Genet, Jean *Treasures of the Night*

Ginsberg, Allen & Orlovsky, Peter *Straight Hearts Delight: Love Poems and Selected Letters*

Peterson, Robert *What Dillinger Meant to Me*

Piercy, Marge *Circles on the Water*

Drama

Browne, Alan *Forty Deuce*

Helbing, Terry (editor) *Directory of Gay Plays*

Morris, Sidney *If This Isn't Love*

Wilson, Doric *Street Theater*

Fierstein, Harvey *Torch Song Trilogy*

Contemporary gay and lesbian fiction

Andrews, Terry (pseudonym) *The Story of Harold*

Barnes, Djuna *Ryder*

Caffrey, John *The Coming Out Party*

Caminha, Adolfo *Bom-Crioulo*

Cameron, Anne *The Journey*

Carney, William *The Rose Exterminator*

Chambers, Jane *Burning*

Curzon, Daniel *From Violent Men*

Curzon, Daniel *Human Warmth & Other Stories*

Diaman, N.A. *Ed Dean is Queer*

Diaman, N.A. *Second Crossing*

Esser, Kevin *Streetboy Dreams*

Fisher, Pete *Special Teachers Special Boys*

Garden, Nancy *Annie on My Mind*

Genet, Jean *Querelle*

Grahn, Judy (editor) *True Life Adventure Stories* Vol. 1

Hamilton, Wallace *Coming Out*

Hamilton, Wallace *Kevin*

Hansen, Joseph *Death Claims*

Herron, Bob *Moritz*

Kent, Girard *The Boy Harlequin and Other Stories*

Kirkwood, James *P.S. Your Cat is Dead*

Koertge, Noretta *Who Was That Masked Woman*

Levy, Owen *A Brother's Touch*

Leyland, Winston (editor) *My Deep Dark Pain is Love*

Leyland, Winston (editor) *Now the Volcano*

Maugham, Robin *The Boy from Beirut: and Other Stories*

Maugham, Robin *Enemy*

Merrick, Gordon *An Idol for Others*

Merrick, Gordon *Forth Into Light*

Merrick, Gordon *The Lord Won't Mind*

Merrick, Gordon *Now Let's Talk About Music*

Merrick, Gordon *One for the Gods*

Merrick, Gordon *Perfect Freedom*

Merrick, Gordon *The Quirk*

Mitchell, Larry *Terminal Bar*

Monette, Paul *Taking Care of Mrs Carroll*

Murdoch, Royal *The Disrobing*

Nelson, Charles *The Boy Who Picked the Bullets Up*

Picano, Felice *Slashed to Ribbons in the Defence of Love: And Other Stories*

Preston, John *Mister Benson*

Rechy, John *The Vampires*

Rumaker, Michael *My First Satyrnalia*

Snyder, Anne *Counter Play*

Stevenson, Richard *Death Trick*

Torchia, Joseph *The Kryptonite Kid*

Vidal, Gore *A Thirsty Evil*

Virga, Vincent *A Comfortable Corner*

Virga, Vincent *Gaywick*

Vojir, Dan *The Sunny Side of Castro Street*
Warren, Patricia Nell *The Front Runner*
Wilson, Carter *Treasures on Earth*
Zapata, Luis *Adonis Garcia*

Erotic fiction and autobiography

Andros, Phil (pseudonym of Samuel Steward, friend of Gertrude Stein) *Below the Belt and Other Stories*

Andros, Phil (pseudonym of Samuel Steward) *My Brother, My Self*

Andros, Phil (pseudonym of Samuel Steward) *Roman Conquests*

Camus, Renaud *Tricks: 25 Encounters*

Coriolan, John *Unzipped*

Kelly, Dennis *Chicken*

Wilde, Oscar (attributed to) *Teleny*

First Hand

Cum

Flesh

Sex

Meat

The ones GTW cannot identify

Body Parts

Cross Sections

Male Love

The Winged Dancer

Winter Music

Breathing Room

Cry to Heaven

Motherbound

Index